Calm
in the
Storm

ALSO BY BROTHER PHAP HUU AND JO CONFINO

*Being with Busyness: Zen Ways to Transform
Overwhelm and Burnout*

Calm in the Storm

Zen Ways to Cultivate Stability in an Anxious World

Brother Phap Huu and Jo Confino

Cohosts of the Plum Village podcast *The Way Out Is In*

PARALLAX PRESS
BERKELEY, CALIFORNIA

Parallax Press
PO Box 7355
Berkeley, CA 94707
parallax.org

Parallax Press is the publishing division of
Plum Village Community of Engaged Buddhism, Inc.
© 2025 by Plum Village Community of
Engaged Buddhism and Jo Confino
All rights reserved

Cover illustration by InnaPoka
Cover design by Katie Eberle
Text design by Maureen Forys, Happenstance Type-O-Rama
Author photograph courtesy of Jo Confino

Printed in the United States of America
Printed by Versa Press on FSC-certified paper

"A Present Moment Practice" on pages 149–150
courtesy of Sister Jina, Chan Dieu Nghiem

Parallax Press's authorized representative in the EU and EEA is
SARL Boutique La Bambouseraie Point UH, Le Pey, 24240 Thénac, France
Email: europe@parallax.org

Content guidance: This book explores aspects of healing from trauma and
contains references that may be triggering, including references to self-harm
and suicide. Please read with care.

Disclaimer: The advice in this book is intended for general information
purposes only. Any application of the material set forth in the following pages
is at the reader's discretion and is their sole responsibility.

ISBN 978-0-938077-55-8
Ebook ISBN 978-0-938077-89-3

Library of Congress Control Number: 2025937388

1 2 3 4 5 VERSA 29 28 27 26 25

Your true home is not an abstract idea; it is something you can touch and live in every moment. No one can take it away from you. Other people can occupy your country, they can even put you in prison, but they cannot take away your true home and your freedom.

Zen Master Thich Nhat Hanh

Beings who've succeeded on earth for millions of years, don't seek, and should not require, our approval. They belong as well as we do. We do ourselves no favors by asking whether their existence is worth our while. We are hardly in a position to judge, hurdling and lurching along as we are with no goal, no plan except: bigger, faster, more.

If we had the courage to be honest about it, we would have to admit that whales and birds and apes and all the rest live fully up to everything of which they are capable. And we, regrettably, fall short of doing that. For them, to be is enough. For us in the isolating alienation of our title retreat from Life, nothing is enough. It is strange how dissatisfied we insist on being, when there is so much of the world to know and love.

Carl Safina

Contents

PREFACE   Arriving   ix

CHAPTER 1   What Takes Us Far from Home   1

CHAPTER 2   Our Stories   1

CHAPTER 3   We Are Not Only Our Stories   21

CHAPTER 4   The Calm   47

CHAPTER 5   Through Any Storm   89

CHAPTER 6   Practices to Return Home   131

CHAPTER 7   True Presence   155

    Appreciation   163
    Notes   167
    About the Authors   169
    About *The Way Out Is In* Podcast   173

Preface

Arriving

Welcome, dear friends, to this guide to coming home to ourselves and coming home to life.

Many of us have traveled a long distance from our center, the place where we can accept ourselves as we are and feel stability in an often chaotic world. We live in an age of anxiety; our nervous systems are overloaded. Many of us juggle complex lives and face pressures to do more and be more. Navigating our own lives is difficult enough, but we do so in the context of a world in turmoil. Exponential changes in technology alongside the fraying of political consensus and institutions that have for many decades helped to create social cohesion are challenging our stability and trust. As if this were not enough, we face threats of runaway climate change, ecosystem degradation, and increasing social injustice. This heavy emotional load generates grief and despair—the possible collapse of civilization as we know it has entered our consciousness and the mainstream dialogue.

In these times when everything appears to be in turmoil and we can feel powerless to shape our world, it is important to cultivate calm in the storm. When we are stable in our center, we can develop the capacity and resilience to accompany ourselves and others through these difficult and momentous times. We can respond rather than react or burn out.

This requires taking time to reflect, a habit that is in stark contrast to our current culture of striving, our expectation for constant progress, and a belief that time is money. When we're always looking forward, we sometimes forget to slow down long enough to pay attention to the streams of wisdom passed down to us through many generations that are still as fresh and relevant today as when they first emerged into our collective consciousness.

We have both found great treasures in the 2,600-year-old teachings of the Buddha, which offer valuable pathways to help us face the polycrisis—the convergence of multiple, interconnected crises that amplify each other—with stability and presence. We are grateful for the simple and profound way these teachings have been embodied and transmitted to us by Zen Master Thich Nhat Hanh, our teacher, who is known as "Thay" (an affectionate Vietnamese term for *teacher*). Thay would have said: "There is no path to being calm, calmness is the path. There is no way to stability, stability is the way."

The title of this book is inspired by one of Thay's teachings in which he uses the metaphor of a boat battered by a big storm and in danger of sinking. The passengers and crew on this boat are fearful, they're frantically running from one side of the deck to the other. If everyone panics like this, Thay points out, the ship will surely be lost. If even one person is able to remain calm, however, their stability might be transmitted to others, and then there is a chance the crew of this sinking ship will be able to work together to save the vessel and their own lives.

To start benefiting from Zen practices involves no complexity or esoteric knowledge, nor years of formal training. All that is needed to get going is to take the first mindful breath and then to keep breathing with awareness, to take the first mindful step and then to keep walking. Cultivating calm in the storm is neither a sprint nor a marathon. We can deepen our understanding until our very last breath and share the wisdom we accumulate along the way with others, who can then further develop their own insights and share them in turn with their family, friends, and community. There is no beginning and no end to this path of peace and freedom; we are drops in the eternal river of life.

The Way Out Is In

Our wish in writing this book is to share what we have learned about cultivating calm in the storm with the hope of offering you spiritual sustenance and practical encouragement as you walk your own path. Many people question what it takes to remain hopeful in these difficult times. In this book, we focus our attention on the understanding that while we cannot change the world on our own, we do have the capacity to change ourselves. Tending to our overwhelm or anxiety offers the greatest opportunity to find our own stability; from this place of centeredness, we can reach out into the world and act with fierce, rooted compassion.

It takes visceral knowing, not intellectual understanding, to bring about fundamental change. If we want to see greater kindness in the world, we need to find our own tenderness within. If we want the world to move away from polarization to deeper collaboration, we ourselves need to find ways to listen deeply to those we believe to be the cause of our suffering. If we want others to feel less isolated and lonely, we need to see past our own beliefs about our separation and disconnection.

The wisdom of the Buddha, the essential insight at the heart of this path, is to accept and engage with our suffering rather than think we can go around it. Suffering and peace belong to each other: we must touch our suffering to touch our peace, and once we touch our peace, we are capable of touching our suffering. If we know how to suffer, we suffer less. The foundational power of this truth—the way out is in—is what inspired us to choose it for the title of the podcast we co-host.

The core teaching of the Buddha is the Four Noble Truths. The first truth is to acknowledge the presence of suffering, and the second is to recognize the causes of suffering. Fortunately, the Buddha identified the third and fourth Noble Truths: suffering can be transformed, and there is a path that leads to the cessation of suffering.[1]

People often fall into two disparate camps: eternally optimistic about the future and repressing the difficult circumstances we face, or struck down by a sense of disenchantment and grief. We have benefited from taking the middle path, which is rooted in honesty and deep looking. From this place of calmness, contemplation, and acknowledgment of what is, we can look our challenges directly in the eye, without averting our gaze, and remain steady. From this place of stability, we can see how we want to respond to the difficulties in our own lives and in the world around us. The middle path, the path of stability these pages explore, reminds us that even if we are facing emotional turmoil, we can still enjoy the beauty of a flower blossoming or the smile of a stranger. We have the capacity to hold much more than one feeling. If we can see our suffering and understand it, transformation is possible.

The formidable American poet W. S. Merwin takes this to its ultimate conclusion in his poem "Place"; "On the last day of the world/I would want to plant a tree" he says. "I want the tree that stands/in the earth for the first time/with the sun already/going down….."[2] Even if we face the unimaginable grief of knowing the world will end today, we can still touch the essence of love and life.

Alone, Together: Our Suffering

Lose-Lose

First, the suffering. Western society has encouraged and finessed a perverse, vice-like trap: we are caught between the jaws of a desire to be perfect and feelings of self-loathing. A lose-lose situation. Though many of us do not believe we are good enough, paradoxically we constantly seek to prove that we are. The more we struggle, the more this trap can tighten its grip on us.

Beyond this alienation from ourselves and our inherent worth, we also experience alienation from each other and from Mother Earth. Human relationships have increasingly become transactional, based on competition and a sense of scarcity. Our busyness and experience of overwhelm or even anxiety make it harder to find the time to develop closer friendships. In an age of technologically infused ultra-connectivity, growing numbers of people feel lonely and disconnected from intimacy and love—from each other and from our environment. Rather than feeling a reverence for the natural world, our minds have been corrupted by the feverish demands of a capitalist system that encourages us to see the planet as a mere inanimate resource to be exploited and consumed. The majority of the world's population now live in cities, and many do not have the opportunity to experience nature. Of course, nature is everywhere: even a cell phone contains natural materials taken from the earth, and there is immense value in appreciating the wildness of a dandelion pushing up through a crack in the sidewalk. Yet *nature* here refers to landscapes not extensively developed by humans, to the unique and increasingly rare experience of moving through a place not defined by humans, places where a larger-than-human perspective looks you in the eyes.

We are not comfortable in ourselves, we are not comfortable with each other, and we are not comfortable on our planet. This experience of being untethered from an innate sense of belonging can generate a toxic cocktail of emotions, ranging from helplessness and hopelessness to betrayal and anger. In this agitated state, we seek to create a sense of calm by trying to take back control and protect our self-esteem. We are like wanderers who feel we do not belong, and we therefore often buy into the idea that a particular product, experience, or lifestyle will allow us to be ourselves and feel part of this world.

The Storm Is Raging

While we know the facts and figures, it is worth deeply connecting to the simple fact that human civilization has been changing at an extraordinary and unrelenting pace since the industrial revolution only 260 years ago. Just compare this with the relatively slow speed of human development over the previous 600,000 years.

Before the industrial revolution began in the 1760s, most people stayed close to the place they were born for their entire lives. Their days were largely spent within their extended families and the local community; most people lived close to the land, their days carved out by the changing seasons. Faith and religion gave a greater sense of meaning and direction. The economy was largely local—most people had few material goods and few ambitions. News traveled slowly, and there was little knowledge of what was going on in the outside world. Life was slower and simpler.

It is important not to see the past through rose-tinted glasses: life then was extremely limited and there was immense suffering related to short life expectancy, extreme poverty, and a lack of freedom of movement or expression. Life in the modern era is in many ways far better—more people, particularly in the West, enjoy longer life expectancy, a higher standard of living, and greater freedom. But we pay a considerable emotional and spiritual cost; we have veered perilously to the other extreme and our pursuit of comfort and freedom generates pain and destruction for other people and other species.

It is an especially difficult time to be young. Many teenagers, particularly in the West, are experiencing whiplash from the relentless demands to fit particular ways of looking or behaving. Flooded by images and videos of people experiencing so-called perfect moments, it is hard not to feel one's own life is imperfect at best. Fear of being judged or even canceled on social media for placing one word or one foot out of place can mean being in a near-constant state of high alert.

Stopping and resting have become luxuries many people feel are often beyond their grasp. We are no longer in tune with the changes of seasons: we are expected to be just as productive in the winter as in the spring. Just imagine if the rest of nature had to operate in this way! It is exhausting and unsustainable. Even if we are able to slow down and stop, we often feel guilty or our minds start clamoring for action. Quietness is often equated with boredom. Annual holidays tend to be about recuperation rather than relaxation, and we see many examples of people getting ill as soon as they go on vacation because their bodies and minds have been so stressed. Rather than savoring our successes, we move immediately to the next thing on our to-do list. We see this across the corporate world, where teams complain there is no time to celebrate one goal being achieved before the next challenge lands on their plates.

This already fast pace of change continues to quicken. Technological advancements, such as AI, are exponential in nature. The flood of fake news and images is making it increasingly difficult to discern what is real and what we can trust. We are outsourcing our knowledge and understanding of the world to ChatGPT and Google. While we may be becoming cleverer, wisdom lags far behind.

Social cohesion is fraying and, in some cases, has unraveled. We often do not know our neighbors, never mind the place our ancestors came from. In our wish to be independent, we often experience less contact with our families and communities. With the diminishment of traditional religion, many people are no longer grounded by a spiritual practice. The free market and consumerism have rushed in to fill this void, and the vacuum has created an extremely narrow view of success and happiness by which we value and judge ourselves and others. The broader context of our essential humanity often ends up on the cutting room floor.

We are witnessing the emergence of an existential crisis. Even a decade ago, climate change for many felt like an abstract idea that was merely to be understood intellectually via facts and figures. But now the impacts of extreme weather have reached our doorsteps. We see daily the impacts of fires, flooding, and droughts, and we know there is potentially far worse to come. The ecosystems on which our lives and wellbeing depend are degrading mercilessly—in just the last fifty years alone, there has been a catastrophic 73 percent decline in the average size of monitored wildlife populations.

The Gift of Death

Our dread of civilizational collapse is forcing us, whether we know it or not, to touch our own mortality. Many (if not most) of us wish to avoid the fact that we will one day die. Our various responses to the polycrisis can, in part, be explained by the insights social anthropologist Ernest Becker shared in his 1970s Pulitzer Prize–winning book, *The Denial of Death*. Becker's work inspired the development of terror management theory, which explores how we tend to respond to threats to our established way of seeing the world (including threats to our own denial of death) by belittling those with different views, seeking to convert our perceived opponents to our own belief system, or responding with physical violence to annihilate our enemies. As we increasingly seek refuge in our own echo chambers, there are profound repercussions for the political sphere: we are experiencing increased polarization.

Buddhist teachings offer an alternative path, helping us to understand there is no need to fear our mortality. We can understand that we are part of a stream of life stretching back to the beginning of time and into the infinite future. We are each one drop in the eternal river of life.

Joanna Macy, a longtime environmental activist, Buddhist scholar, and deep ecologist, speaks eloquently to the possibility of death even being a gift: "Death walks with us, and that is the great mystery," she said as a guest on our podcast. "I love the way it's put in the writings of the Dharma: death is certain, but the time of death is uncertain. It's a double whammy. You are going to die and you don't know when. It could be in five minutes or fifty years. This keeps us kind of on an edge of presence. We are on borrowed time, and this gives us a quality of being able to be present and in the now—because it's all we know we have. It's really all we have."[3]

Rather than seeing those with opposing views as our enemies, we have the option of looking through the lens of interbeing. When we do this, we see that we are not individual separate selves; at the core, all our lives are deeply intertwined. On a fundamental level, we all want to transform our suffering, but the way we each seek to do this is determined by numerous different causes and conditions: our ancestral patterns, our parenting, our environment, our society, and our own lived experience. Our individual beliefs and perceptions about the world and how we want it to be all come from the same source: a desire to experience ease and well-being.

PREFACE

BREATHER

When we don't see the self as self,
What do we have to fear?
See the world as your self.
Have faith in the way things are.
Love the world as your self;
Then you can care for all things

from the Tao Te Ching,
translated by Stephen Mitchell[4]

CHAPTER 1

What Takes Us Far from Home

Before we can find our way home to ourselves, we must first understand what has taken us away. We'd like to begin by looking gently and honestly at the forces—both internal and external—that pull us away from our center and keep us running frantically to and fro when a storm threatens to sink our ship. These are not failures or flaws, but learned patterns and protective strategies that helped us survive in the past. Perfectionism, the relentless pursuit of achievement, disconnection from nature, the inability to see our own worth—these are habits born from fear, from wounding, and from a society that often measures us by impossible standards.

Many of us have forgotten how to rest. We've become strangers to stillness, untrusting of silence, uneasy with simply being. We've been taught we must prove our value through doing, that love must be earned, and that there's always a better version of ourselves just out of reach. In that striving, we lose touch with the profound truth: we are already enough. We already belong.

None of this is about blaming ourselves for the distance we've traveled from home, from our stability, but about naming that distance with clarity and compassion. Only by seeing what clouds our vision can we begin to clear the way. These reflections are not meant to create judgment, but to spark curiosity. What beliefs have we inherited? What patterns are we ready to loosen? What if the ease we've been searching for has been within us all along—quiet, patient, waiting to be remembered?

Perfectionism

JO CONFINO: One of the stories we often tell ourselves is that we need to strive for perfection. But if we stop to look, we can see the search for perfectionism will, by its nature, end in failure. Islamic artists are known to include imperfections in their works to signify that only God has the ability to be perfect. Within the Japanese Zen art of *wabi sabi* is the practice of *kintsugi*, in which broken pottery is repaired using gold powder and lacquer. Rather trying to hide defects, the application of gold highlights the extraordinary beauty of imperfection and impermanence.

Life is to be lived, not to be solved. We can allow our scars to shine instead of trying to cover them up. Rather than being uncomfortable with uncertainty, we can enjoy the mystery. Rather than seeing paradoxes as conundrums to be resolved, we can see them as reference points for going deeper into the not knowing.

Perfectionism is an attempt to control life. It is often driven by feelings of shame and judgment. If only we can reach a mythical endpoint, we believe, then we can feel happy and accepted. It is fool's gold and ends up exacerbating the very feelings we are trying to escape.

One of the last times I interviewed Thay for *The Guardian*, he shared that the search for perfection should be replaced with the wish to see life as an endless learning journey. "In Buddhism, we speak of love as something limitless," he told me.

> The four elements of love—loving kindness, compassion, joy, and equanimity—have no frontier. That is true with your practice, your achievement. We don't need to be perfect. That's the good thing to know: you don't need to be perfect. If you're making a little bit of progress toward a little bit more peace and joy every day, that's good enough. Thay continues to practice and his insights grow deeper every day.
>
> It's like the teaching of *I have arrived, I am home*, which came to me many decades ago; it is still deepening. If Thay has this body for another hundred years, he will continue to practice like that, to learn how to love better, to understand better. There's no limit to the practice. I think

that is true for the human race: we can continue to learn, generation after generation. I think it's time for us to begin to learn how to love in non-discriminative ways because we are intelligent enough, but we are not loving enough.

There is great beauty in wanting to give our very best to who we are and what we do. But the search for perfection is often based in fear. What our logical mind finds hard to grasp is that our tendency is to keep feeding the fear rather than calming it. By reaching for something that is out of our reach, we continue to believe we do not have what it takes to fully succeed in life; we feel neither calm nor stable. We can use perfectionism as an excuse to not even start particular projects because we believe we will end up humiliating ourselves. By constantly believing there is another mountain we need to climb, we are unable to fully enjoy this present moment.

But if we stop to reflect, we can start to see that it is often we ourselves who choose the standards we wish to attain. We can change that. Even if there's an authority figure who complains about what we are doing, we choose how we want to respond. Often, when powerful people criticize us, their criticism is the result of their own psychological wounds.

One of the senior nuns in Plum Village, a deep thinker and an advanced Zen practitioner, shared that she still sometimes catches herself saying aloud "Stupid girl, stupid girl" when she doesn't succeed in something. It is such an old pattern, transmitted by her mother, that she continues to repeat it despite knowing logically that such words are neither fair nor true. Sometimes our minds can self-sabotage.

A woman in her twenties whom I coached shared that she was keen to take part in a triathlon, an endurance race consisting of swimming, cycling, and running. But she had convinced herself not to enter because of the perceived risk that she would fail to complete the course and would feel humiliated. She had been seeking to project a more positive scenario, trying to convince herself she was being too negative and that it was entirely possible she would be able to complete the circuit. But this attempt to calm her fears through logic alone was not enough to break through her emotional barriers.

When we looked into the root causes of her aversion to risk, she recognized that two experiences of being bullied as a young girl had made her avoid situations in which she didn't feel in control because she never again wanted to feel the intense humiliation she had experienced as a six-year-old. Of course, this didn't just relate to sport but to all aspects of her life. It was more important to the hurt child within to keep herself safe than to explore a situation in which immediate success was not certain.

We worked at reframing her unease, uncovering that the reason she most loves being active is she can touch the present moment and remove all distractions from her mind. She can feel free. After recognizing this, she came to understand that taking part in the triathlon was more important than finishing. I suggested that if she didn't succeed the first time for whatever reason, she could learn from the experience and try again when she was more prepared. To me, it was the most obvious thing to say, but this simple acknowledgement changed her whole perspective. Her inner critic had told her it was essential she succeed on the first attempt in everything she did to avoid feeling humiliated. She hadn't even considered that she could view a triathlon as a process of learning and development.

Of course, she is by no means alone. So many of us are locked in a feeling of not being good enough. Sometimes it is because of a past trauma, but it can also be as a result of having high expectations in many cases transmitted by our parents, education, friends, and social media. Let's be honest: there's a lot of anxiety floating around out there.

Many parents, for example, see their own value as based on their children's successes at school, in their careers, and in the relationships they choose. By holding such high standards, they are setting up their children for a life of constant pressure and feelings of not being enough. It is also true that many children grow up neglected by their parents or without the educational opportunities afforded to others. This too can lead to feelings of inadequacy and a belief that even modest success is impossible. It can take great courage to step out from under this shadow, especially if there is a lack of support in the form of mentors or attentive teachers.

PHAP HUU: When we really look at perfectionism, it's a crazy notion. Like, what even *is* perfect? Is the idea of perfection somebody who is very successful, knows all the answers, can weather any storm, and shoulder any responsibility? What perfection tends to block is the importance of vulnerability, being in touch with our softer side, our humility and willingness to make mistakes and apologize for any missteps.

For instance, I see this in the art of t'ai chi. Moving through the flow of the various steps, we see that letting go of one movement can add strength to the next movement. This is very different from taekwondo, the Korean martial art, which is very firm, strong, with a lot of kicks. To go from taekwondo to learning t'ai chi, I had to almost unlearn in order to expand, to see the ease, well-being, and strength in this new way of movement. Using this metaphor, I see how taekwondo represents the harshness in our drive for perfection and t'ai chi shows us the power of softness.

In our times, it is essential to smile to the imperfection inside of us. It can be a joy to say *I made a mistake* or *I need to apologize*, because that's a flower in action. When we've done something we know has caused suffering, we have the capacity to acknowledge that and then to begin anew, to apologize, to say *I'm so sorry, I was very unmindful. I wasn't aware of the words I used and the energy I carried.* Being vulnerable like this allows me to learn and grow without shame and strengthens my relationship with the other person, who will also feel relieved. Tenderness and compassion in mainstream society can be considered weaknesses, but part of the journey back to our center, to calm and stability in the storm of fear and anxiety, is self-compassion. Self-compassion becomes the base that allows us to accept ourselves, to accept our unwholesome actions, and to find the beauty in our imperfection.

Even if we have made a mistake, we can recognize all the other wonderful qualities we have. We have to ask ourselves again and again and again, "Have we arrived? Are we home yet?" Every day we are asked to learn to arrive, to learn to be at home. What is so beautiful is that as we progress on the path of life, our definition of home continues to evolve—our way of being in the present moment deepens.

Competition

PHAP HUU: There is such a strong sense of competition in the West, both in the education system and in our concept of success. We are told to have more and to be more accomplished. More than whom? Perhaps someone different from us, someone with different beliefs or political leanings, or someone who has made us suffer. There is a feeling of always running, either toward something or after something. There is a projection we each receive just growing up in our society: we have to do more to get more.

We have to do better; it's a way of paying our respect to our parents. I speak as someone from a different ethnicity, who grew up in a society in which white people were the majority. A big part of my upbringing was influenced by the wish to become very rich so I could give back to my parents and show my gratitude for everything they went through as refugees from Vietnam. I had the mindset of wanting to gain more; achievement meant I had to be better than who I was already. I was programmed, in a way, to sprint forward.

There is also a competition to look good, related to an aversion to not being accepted by others. I recognized this tendency when I came to Plum Village, where for the first time in my teenage life I didn't have to care so much about my own appearance. Every day back home, the first thing I did after waking up was my hair—it was far more important than eating breakfast. Spiky hair was the cool style then, and I used a good fifteen to twenty minutes doing my hair, putting on a lot of gel. I spent a lot of energy cultivating my appearance in order to feel I would be accepted. I remember waking up in Plum Village and realizing I didn't have to do my hair, I could wear the same clothes as the day before, and I would still be accepted. I had this feeling of being very safe. Just seeing everyone's smiles, being able to look at someone I didn't really know and smile at them and appreciate their presence, was very new. I came as a child, a young teenager, and this simple way of greeting each other was the first time I experienced what it was like to just be with a group of people without having to earn their acceptance.

JO CONFINO: After speaking with young people today, I look at my own youth, and it feels like a bygone age. The emotional landscape is in many ways the same, but the speed and scale of change is so different. Growing up, I felt very insecure about my looks—I was short for my age, which made me feel small inside of myself. Being from a family with not much money, I wore hand-me-downs from my elder brothers and had no ability to follow any of the fashions. At school I was jealous of the in-crowd; I had a longing to be like them, all the time knowing they were out of my league. And yet, my orbit of experience was geographically and psychologically boundaried by my school and my friends. I had little awareness of the wider world: no mobile phone, no computer, no social media, no 24/7 news. So, although I suffered, the scale of my world made it more manageable.

That is so different from today's experience growing up, which seems like my life on steroids *and* psychedelics. It's hard to feel cozy and at peace when there are so many demands from the hyper-capitalistic, hyper-sexualized, hyper-consumerist society coming at us from so many directions. People are expected to fit in in so many ways. Young people are now expected to be everything, everywhere, all at once—to be their unique selves, find their true vocation, and live up to their highest potential.

When society demands so much of us and we feel we are not able to make the grade, that can be deeply painful and invoke intense anxiety. It is no wonder some young people turn to eating disorders or self-harm in an attempt to exert some sort of control over their lives.

Phap Huu: I also had a complex because I was short: if only I could be a little bit taller, everything would be okay. These complexes feel very real and drag us down the rabbit hole of not-enoughness. It's very painful. As a monk, I've learned that beauty is not on the outside. I aspire to have inner freedom.

Yes, there are conditions that are outside of our control, but we have the ability to see each other as flowers in the garden of humanity. Imagine if all of us were the same, how boring life on earth would be. Imagine there were only oak trees—there would be no fruit to eat, right? And imagine if there were only apples—we could never enjoy a durian. The diversity of the planet can be a mirror for us and help us see the beauty of difference.

When someone trains to become a monastic, one of the ten novice precepts they take is not to wear jewelry and cosmetics to enhance their appearance; we redefine beauty to be inner beauty, our inner freedom. That is the beauty that outlasts the impermanence of our bodies.

We have a practice called the Five Remembrances that can be very supportive in remembering we're all human beings and that one day we will all get sick and die. Outer beauty is fleeting, but inner beauty transcends space and time.

> I am of the nature to grow old. There is no way to escape growing old.
> I am of the nature to have ill-health. There is no way to escape having ill-health.
> I am of the nature to die. There is no way to escape death.
> All that is dear to me and everyone I love are of the nature to change. There is no way to escape being separated from them.
> I inherit the results of my actions of body, speech, and mind. My actions are my continuation.[5]

The Five Remembrances are a reminder of the impermanent nature of life, a reminder of what is important: how we think, talk, and act. These are the things that ripple out into the world and have real impact, even after our lives have ended. For example, the magnetism of Thay's simple practice of walking meditation during retreats always captivated me. All the children wanted to hold his hand and sit around him, yet he was quiet the whole time. He expressed beauty in his way of being, his way of moving freely on this planet and transforming the pain and suffering of his experiences without being caught by them. He walked with steps of freedom in this present moment, not taking for granted this moment of joy, of peace, of connection.

Those of us who are young are constantly going to be tackling the question, *Am I enough?* Even those of us who are older still have these types of doubts. Let us collectively transform this together so we can transmit to the next generation the realization that we are all enough.

Striving

PHAP HUU: Often, striving is an attempt to run away from our current situation. We compete against ourselves and against those around us. Our striving and grasping can even extend into love, seeking to show we love another person more in order to gain more attention. At the root of this behavior is whether or not we have a path.

In Zen, we say if you don't have a direction, you are a hungry ghost—all you want is to grab the light and love around you. A Zen teacher will give someone who is lost a direction and will help them find a path to walk.

Many people get confused by the teachings of Buddhism—that they encourage people to let go of their desires and not have goals while simultaneously advocating for volition and aspirations. It is important to be clear: somebody who has no will to live, no direction, and no path is very lost and suffers deeply. They carry the energy of loneliness, the energy of laziness, and the energy of feeling rootless. But when you have a path, this is when you apply the insight of aimlessness, the insight to slow down, and the insight to enjoy the path you're walking in the present moment.

Striving is the energy of projecting ourselves into the future. But Thay once said something that woke me up. "You know what's in the future? It's your graveyard. So why rush there?" When we're young, we already want to be eighteen and independent, to do whatever we want. And then when we're older, we all want to be younger. We're such confused human beings. We always want something else. We're always trying to run after what we're not. Mindfulness is to recognize and accept who you are now.

People these days have been educated to believe they can be happy only when they have achieved a goal; so, they'll keep running after goals. This sense that happiness must be earned has unfortunately leaked into the world of spiritual seekers. I'm sure many of us started exploring the spiritual dimension because we were suffering. We meet the teachings when we come up against an insurmountable wall in life and aren't able to find a way through it or around it. Yet the energy of striving can arise when we come into direct contact with spiritual teachings; for example, when people visit Plum Village monastery, they see monks, nuns, and lay practitioners at peace with themselves, at ease and present, and they may immediately want to strive to become like that.

It's wonderful to recognize that you wish to have peace in your life, but it's important to grow your trust that you can embody it yourself slowly rather than trying to grab hold of it like someone in fear of drowning desperately grabbing hold of a bit of flotsam. If you have never received love, if you've never seen someone who is truly solid and stable, you may not understand that this way of being is achievable. In Zen, we speak about recognizing the teacher in yourself and learning to trust that teacher in you. It is important to experience it for yourself—this means developing trust and having faith in our own capacity, not always looking for calm, stability, or happiness outside of ourselves or in the presence of a spiritual teacher. This insight can help water down your striving. Insight comes from awareness and practicing mindfulness. We practice, and we have baby insights to have a big insight.

Mindfulness is, first, just to be who you are and accept who you are. This is the first baby enlightenment we all can achieve. Accepting who you are, you may start to look inside and explore yourself, to be curious. Be sure to also ask yourself: What am I grateful for in myself? Recognize the energies and habits that bring you suffering; do not shy away from them. Acceptance is an act of love. When we accept ourselves, we will have transformative insights. Insight liberates us. It is enough to know we are offering the best we can today from right where we are, to recognize with ease that sometime in the future we will have advanced our understanding. This is the beauty of growth. Insight is not to be used to compete against one another.

I was recently asked, what's my favorite season? While I enjoy them all, spring and autumn have the most meaning for me. In the springtime, nature is reborn. New leaves form, buds manifest, and you get to see the unfolding journey of a tree, of a plant, of a flower. In the autumn, trees and plants know how to preserve their energy and survive the winter—they shed their leaves and store nutrients for the following year. I invite all of us to look at our spiritual path like that. There are going to be moments of growth, of blossoming, when we are full of energy and feel motivated, ready to be at the frontline of any suffering and embrace it, transform it. And there will be moments when a harsh winter is coming and we need to close our doors to keep the warmth inside. We need to take a step back. We need to say no. This is not giving up.

Sometimes we think we should always move forward, but sometimes moving backward is moving forward. There's a saying in Vietnamese, "Take a step back to take two steps forward later." We have to give ourselves a new view of spiritual growth. Maturity is not to always be solid as a mountain, to be as spacious as the sky. Sometimes it's just to learn to be still and to accept what is there.

Thay would tell us to look at a photo of ourselves when we were much younger and to ask, "Am I the same now or am I different?" We do not need to judge or compare. We can feel deep appreciation for that youthfulness, for all the conditions that have given me the insights that led to who I am today. I can then appreciate the pain and the suffering I experienced—it has taught me suffering is real; therefore, I don't want to repeat that suffering, and I don't want to give the suffering I received to others around me. To look into the past is to educate ourselves and to learn.

I've reflected a lot on my habit of striving and my meditation sometimes is just to check in with myself. What am I competing against? What am I trying to run away from? At the same time, don't try to be exactly the same as before. See what nourishes you in this moment. Don't use your striving to attack yourself. Sometimes our habits, our energies, are there for us to reflect on and learn from. If I don't have striving energy, maybe I don't have any aspirations. This is where the insight of interbeing comes into play—not having a dualistic view can help us wake up.

The Weight of Pleasing Others

PHAP HUU: One thing I've grown out of is the wish to *make* other people happy; to be a people pleaser. Of course, there is an element of interbeing when somebody else is happy—it can also lift your spirits. But when you do not recognize your own happiness, you will never feel fulfilled.

When I ask myself what changes I've made since becoming a monk, I see I have more clarity about where I invest my energy, and I see myself letting go of the expectation that everybody should be happy. This wish to please others goes back to my childhood; I always wanted my family to be happy, and sometimes we weren't. There was a vast hole there, and when I saw my family struggle, I ran after their happiness. Now, as I practice, I can recognize that this energy is still there, but I embrace it much more and accept other people's suffering. I give others the space to transform and do not try to make them transform right away or to do it for them.

By wanting people to change, we force our views on them, and that causes a lot of suffering—for the other person and for yourself. When you put your dreams and happiness on another person, if they don't change, you can feel a failure. You are also likely to end up feeling progressively less compassionate toward the person you want to support. Your heart grows smaller rather than bigger. Understanding the core of our desire to people-please can go a long way toward cultivating a lasting sense of calm and stability.

BREATHER

"To be beautiful means to be yourself. You don't need to be accepted by others. You need to accept yourself. When you are born a lotus flower, be a beautiful lotus flower, don't try to be a magnolia flower. If you crave acceptance and recognition and try to change yourself to fit what other people want you to be, you will suffer all your life. True happiness and true power lie in understanding yourself, accepting yourself, having confidence in yourself."

—Thich Nhat Hanh [6]

CHAPTER 2

Our Stories

The power of stories has been central to human experience since the dawn of civilization. We learn about ourselves and others by being attentive to both the stories we tell and the web of stories we hear. By reflecting on what we share and what we choose to keep secret, we learn about the way our minds work, where we may be fearful and stuck, and where our consciousness is evolving. Yet we can also get caught in our stories; there is a balance to find between honoring our stories and giving ourselves permission to drop them when they no longer serve us, when it's time to send new stories into the world.

We'd like to offer the personal stories of our sufferings—of what has tested our trust and faith in the world and the pathways we have taken to face these challenges and come back to our centers. We hope you can connect to the energy of our words, even if your own experiences feel very divergent. For each of us, our journeys through life have many ups and downs, moments of illumination as well as major setbacks. Rather than viewing this lack of smooth progress with frustration, the two of us have learned to see this path as an ever-changing kaleidoscope of color and texture.

We Are All Refugees

We are both children of refugees who fled their home countries due to war and persecution. Our parents were faced with the challenge of building new lives in countries where they had no roots and little economic security. In our own lifetime experience, we have felt the ripples of this trauma in ways both obvious and subtle, some of which have only come into our conscious awareness in recent years. In our childhoods, this trauma manifested in the deep pain of not feeling part of mainstream society and in the desperate wish to be accepted, to feel we were enough.

While our stories are unique in their own way, through our interactions with the many people we support as spiritual mentors, we have found that much of the emotional turbulence we have both encountered is not ours alone. We all have a refugee somewhere inside of us, even if it is hidden from view.

For many millions of people every year, being a refugee is literally their day-to-day experience. Extreme events such as war, gender, racial and religious discrimination, as well as climate-related catastrophes such as drought, flooding, and fire are forcing increasing numbers of people to physically uproot themselves. There are myriad other reasons people may need to find a new place to rest their heads, ranging from divorce and domestic violence to economic hardships caused by an increasingly unstable global economy.

This displacement can often give rise to a deep sense of loss, alienation, and loneliness. In some cases, refugees suffer further discrimination in the new places they settle because of their hosts' fears that their own local culture is being swamped and a sense that local communities no longer feel like home.

Even those who have enjoyed a stable outer world may suffer from a tormented inner world that prevents them from living in peace. We can feel like refugees inside our minds and inside our bodies. Wealth, fame, and sensual pleasures cannot paper over life's difficulties—often, such pursuits exacerbate an underlying anxiety.

In a bid to escape our suffering and our fear of death, our minds concoct various strategies, such as perfectionism: we become people pleasers or seek to manage our lives and the lives of others to the nth degree. Increasing numbers of people lose themselves through addictions of one kind or another. We can also get caught in spiritual bypassing, pretending everything is okay by using words such as *compassion* and *forgiveness* without being connected to their deep meaning or purpose—this leads to repression and denial, rather than acceptance and freedom.

Brother Phap Huu: Healing the Inner Child

The Wounded Child

PHAP HUU: We all have a child within us that is wounded—the child reminds us of those elements of our past that need reflection and attention. Even though our practice in Zen is to learn to dwell in the present moment and not be carried away by the future or be swept away by the past, when we meditate, we need to know how to deeply touch our historical suffering with compassion. If we don't transform it, we will unwittingly offer the same suffering to whoever is close to us.

My family were refugees from the war in Vietnam and eventually settled in Canada. My father was a boat person, and then he experienced a really tough time in a refugee camp. And of course, if you can't handle the deep suffering of being uprooted from your home in this way, then you find ways to express it that are not always skillful—often through emotions such as frustration and anger as well as behaviors like excessive drinking. As children, we're so pure; we just suck in all of the suffering of our parents, and it becomes a part of who we are. It was that way with me and my father.

I grew up in a Buddhist family. Ancestor worship is part of our tradition and history. Every day before going to school, my parents instructed me to light a stick of incense and put it on our family altar. I did not understand the deeper meaning of this daily ritual; I just did it because I was an obedient child. Finally, one day I got fed up with this tradition and said to myself that I no longer wanted to light incense. It seemed to have no relevance to my life in Canada.

Years later, when I came to Plum Village for the first time, I took part in one particular celebration—the Rose Ceremony—that honors our moms and our dads. In that ceremony, which Thay created in 1983, we begin by lighting incense to light up our gratitude toward our parents. If our parents are still alive, we then receive a red rose. If one of our parents has passed away, we receive a white rose to pin on our jacket or shirt. In that ceremony, supported by the collective energy of the community, I was able to reflect on how much my parents had sacrificed for me to be here: to have moved to Canada, to be in Plum Village in France for the occasion of the ceremony, and to be alive at all. My father made the decision to leave Vietnam to find a better future for his family. I was able to truly see all the suffering and struggles he went through just for me to live in a society and country with more safety and freedom.

I hadn't grown up with that understanding. But suddenly, when I was in the ceremony talking about remembering our parents' sacrifices, my heart filled with gratitude. All the mistakes and suffering within our family suddenly became very small; I was able to see the bigger picture of what they had offered us.

As I've grown older, I have come to recognize that rather than believing I'm a victim of my parents' struggles, I have the ability to help transform that suffering for them. As a child, I remember seeing some behaviors in my father that I didn't like. I promised myself, *When I grow up, I'm never going to be like that*. But one day, I suddenly recognized that I was acting exactly like my dad. I recognized that I shouldn't expect my dad to transform that behavior; first I can transform it in myself—the right conditions may not have been present in this lifetime for him to be able to change.

> *"If you ever have difficulties with your parents, please do not think that they don't love you. Maybe some mistakes or difficulties in their past created layers of suffering that weighed down and obscured that love. We know if anything did happen to us, our parents would cry all their tears. And if something happened to our mother or father, we would also cry until our eyes turn red. We should recognize that they themselves must have had a lot*

of suffering and difficulties. They suffer, and haven't been able to transform that suffering, so they transmit that suffering to their children. We are no different. We suffer because of misunderstandings, because of anger; and as a result, we may also have accidentally spoken unkind words or reacted unkindly to our mother and father."

Thich Nhat Hanh

Bullying

Growing up together in Canada, one of my cousins was full of anger, and he bullied me for what seemed like no reason. This was a source of great pain in my childhood. When I joined the monastic community as a young teenager, I realized I still held a lot of fear inside. I am on the short side, and my fear was directed toward a few monks, in particular, a strongly built, six-foot-tall monastic who resembled my cousin. Whenever I saw him, I shrank a little, feeling scared for no real reason. These dynamics were buried so deep in me that it took four years in the monastery before I could identify my inferiority complexes and call them by their true name.

Thay teaches that we all have a hurt young child inside us; it is important to turn toward and listen to that child. They are like a wound telling you that healing is needed. I learned from Thay to communicate with the child within and tell him that now we have a chance to heal. We are grown-ups: we have the right to protect ourselves; we know how to speak out; we know how to be stable. We can learn how to care for our happiness, to cultivate our joy, our compassion, and our understanding—that young child needs all of this. They need to be treated with tenderness, to be embraced, to know they are okay now. This is why it is so important to know how to nourish our well-being and our sense of safety, for example with meditation.

I remember telling the young child inside, "Everyone around you now, especially in Plum Village, is very kind. They are not here to harm you. They're here to just be with you on this path." It sounds so simple, but in that moment of meditating with the wounded child inside of me, I felt a breakthrough. I remember feeling so much lighter, so much more free. It wasn't the end, though—we have habits and marks of fear that need to slowly be transformed. From time to time, I *still* recognize an unnecessary fear-based reaction in my body. When this happens, I sense the presence of the young child within and I remind myself that it's okay to embrace him, to be there for him. That child is still present, but he is so much stronger, so much wiser, contained within the adult me.

There's an even deeper practice: recognizing that any person who caused us harm as a young child must themselves have experienced intense suffering to behave in such a way. When we remember this, we can have a little more understanding; perhaps we can even dare to have compassion. This practice has helped me to forgive my cousin—for my own sake, for my own growth—and to forgive myself for my own reactions in those moments, my perceived weakness. Through that process, I learned to forgive a lot of people.

I'm lucky to be able to draw on my mother when I practice forgiveness. She is very kind and understanding—these qualities have been transmitted to me through her way of taking care of me as a child, for which I'm deeply grateful. Her example helps me to practice forgiveness, which can sometimes still be quite difficult.

The cousin who bullied me now has children. I think if I had not become a monk and met the Buddhist teachings, I may have behaved angrily toward my nephews and nieces, his children. But because I have been able to understand and forgive him inside of me, I've been able to stop that cycle of hate. When I see his children, I have only love for them, because I've learned that whether we are a parent, an elder brother, an elder sister, an uncle, an aunt, or a friend, our way of being is itself a teaching, far more powerful than anything we might say.

As a young child, one of my responses to being bullied was to feed anger and violence in myself, and I started bullying one of my younger cousins. I did this even though she was an only child and looked toward me and my elder sister as her own siblings—we played together every day. From time to time, I would say something really mean or do something just to make her angry. After recognizing my five-year-old child within and healing him, I called this cousin, whom I had not seen in four or five years, and I apologized. I spoke up and acknowledged something I am not proud of—I felt if I didn't have the courage to express my remorse, she might continue to hold on to the woundedness she'd experienced.

Meditation gives us insight, but we also must have courage to act, to do what is right. The Plum Village tradition is based on the idea of Engaged Buddhism: it's not enough to sit on a cushion and seek enlightenment; we must take our insights out into the world to help others transform their suffering.

Healing and Cultural Heritage

There are many reasons why we may not feel connected to life. Part of my healing has been to learn more about where my family originally came from and explore how I can honor and continue my cultural heritage. Growing up in Canada but knowing my parents were from Vietnam, there were many moments when I didn't want to connect to my own roots. I had a complex—I didn't want to see myself as Vietnamese. We call it "the banana complex": yellow on the outside, but deep down, we want to be white like Westerners.

It was difficult to know where I fit in. It took many years for me to learn that knowing where I'm from—knowing my roots—can be very liberating. I came to realize, *Wow, I'm so rich.* My ancestors created an amazing culture. I want to benefit from it and bring these beautiful qualities to the West. I want elements of where I'm from to manifest in the West in new forms appropriate for this generation. This is the beauty of our world today: we can learn about our cultures through the Internet, by traveling, and by coming back to our roots, and all of these approaches can help us expand our horizons.

I'm not going back in time or trying to be like a person from a different age. But connecting to the past helps me to become more free in the present. I think that many young Vietnamese people who grew up in the West will have to go through this process of coming back to their roots to see the magnificence of their heritage. This groundedness creates so much power, love, understanding, and stability. It is home. When we know ourselves, we have a much better chance of staying calm in whatever storms life may bring.

Jo Confino: Making Peace with the Past

Intergenerational Trauma

JO CONFINO: As I started cowriting this book, I had a recurring dream about starting off on a journey and then encountering many obstacles along the way. In each of the dreams, I came to the edge of a precipice too high to leap from without risking my life. At that moment, someone appeared who could help me to come down safely so I could continue on my journey. These dreams reminded me of Joseph Campbell's seminal book *The Hero With a Thousand Faces*, in which he finds that myths from many cultures share the same fundamental elements—a foundational story seemingly inherited via our collective cultural DNA. This common story involves a hero going on a quest, confronting enormous difficulties, being helped when they most need it, and arriving home transformed, able to confer blessings on others.

I first came across this monomyth as a young man after being inspired by Paulo Coelho's *The Alchemist*. This book tells the story of Santiago, a shepherd boy who dreams of finding a hidden treasure. Santiago goes on a long and arduous quest in search of this treasure, only to discover that it had been buried all along in the place he had started.[7]

I see this myth embedded in my own journey through life. In my early years, I experienced my place in the world in a very rudimentary way: the family I lived with and the house I lived in. On the surface everything looked normal, but on the inside, I felt empty, lonely, and sad. As a young boy, I had little knowledge of the traumas of Nazism and fascism my parents had suffered from, both individually and together, during the Second World War and its aftermath. These included the loss of their eldest daughter Rachel and the discovery that their first son, Moshe, suffered from severe autism as a young child and was placed in a mental institution.

All of this was kept out of sight and out of mind as I grew up. My mother later confided that she'd been advised by parenting experts to lock all the pain behind a closed door and forge a new path forward in their new country. But despite their best intentions, my parents' experiences leached out and formed an undercurrent of sorrow in my life. By now, I've realized that most families have secrets and lies that continue to play out, sometimes over many generations, even if the original causes have been lost in the mists of time.

As I entered my teens, I felt I was sitting at the edge of an ocean of suffering; I felt very much like an outsider in what I considered to be mainstream society. I had little sense of inner resilience and could see myself only through the eyes of others. I felt akin to a social butterfly, gathering a little nourishing pollen from each social interaction before fluttering off to the next flower. But I never felt truly nourished.

In recent years, the discoveries of research into intergenerational trauma—and how events in one person's life can alter not only the expression of their DNA but also affect the next generation through epigenetic changes—has helped me better understand this period of my life. I had failed to locate my sadness in my own life experiences, unable to realize this sadness had been transmitted to me. In the years since I came to understand this, I have seen this phenomenon in coaching clients who have spent years unsuccessfully seeking the cause of their suffering within their own lived experience, only to find it had been passed down to them.

Collapsing Time

In my late twenties, I realized that no amount of love and affection ever filled the aching black hole inside of me. In fact, any attention I received paradoxically made me feel even less worthy—I didn't feel I deserved it.

Similarly to Brother Phap Huu, one of my first healing experiences involved connecting with my inner child. On a reporting assignment in New Orleans, I joined a group of about three hundred people in a three-day workshop held by the well-known therapist and author John Bradshaw, who had hosted many popular self-help series on the PBS television channel. Bradshaw took us on a visualization journey, asking us to close our eyes and imagine walking back to the family home where we grew up, to go inside and find ourselves as a child. I remember going upstairs, entering my old bedroom, and seeing myself as an eight- or nine-year-old child crying my eyes out and feeling very, very alone. When I asked this boy version of myself how he felt, he told me he didn't see any point in carrying on living.

In the intensity of that moment, I recognized a deep disparity between my adult view of my childhood and my lived experience: usually, when we think back to our childhood, we mistakenly view it from an adult's perspective—we contextualize our suffering and forget the raw power of the early experiences we were often unable to share with anyone.

In the visualization, I sat on the bed next to this young version of myself and comforted him. I told him that everything would be okay, that I was here for him, and that this sadness would one day melt away—he would grow up into a beautiful man. This extraordinarily emotional experience collapsed space and time. I felt as if I truly sat there comforting myself while the child within me recognized that I was here to help. The ability to give the child within me love, understanding, and compassion transformed me in ways that resonate to this day.

Later in that workshop, I closed my eyes and an image came to me of standing upright with my head, torso, and legs representing the present moment. Being grounded in this way allowed me to raise my left arm to reach into the past and then to raise my right arm to reach into the future. In that posture, I had the insight that only in the present moment is it possible to reach into the past and heal it. The future, I saw, is not some projected time outside of us, but already located inside of us in the present moment. Our healing in the past can flow into the present and begin to transform the future. Because my child-self now felt safer, I felt safer in the present moment and would feel safer in the future.

Upon returning to New York from New Orleans, I recognized that despite the power of my experience, I needed professional help to better piece together the jigsaw puzzle of my life. I vividly remember going to my initial session with a Jungian analyst. He started by asking me the most basic question: "What do you hope to achieve by coming to see me?" In that safe environment, words flooded out of my mouth like waters from a breaking dam: I told him I had spent my whole life feeling I was at war with myself, and that all I wanted was to find a moment of true peace. Before those words came tumbling out of my mouth on that day, I had not even been aware that I experienced my life in this way. It had been hidden from view, much like my parents' suffering.

While writing this book, I have gone back to a diary I had at that time. There is an entry written in a child-like scrawl by my non-dominant left hand that says: *Dear Jo, I want to come home. I so want to be myself. Show me the way. I've been lost for such a long time. Help me find peace.* It is signed *Jo*. I had suddenly become aware of an inner critic sitting on my shoulder and incessantly whispering in my ear that I was not good enough, criticizing both the decisions I'd made and decisions I wasn't brave enough to make. I'd seen the destructive force of war in the world, but I had not recognized the low-level war going on inside of me, a war with no one to mediate the conflict or negotiate a ceasefire.

I told my therapist during those sessions in New York that I felt like I'd been wandering in a desert all my life with no map and no physical reference points to help guide me. I had no path to walk, not even a sense of direction, like the hungry ghost Brother Phap Huu described earlier.

Friends were confused when I described these encounters with my therapist. To all intents and purposes, I looked happy and successful from the outside. I had a loving relationship, lived in one of the world's most vibrant cities, and I was progressing in my career. Yet I did not know who I was and therefore suffered from anxiety, knowing some inner quality of stability was missing.

Inner Qualities

After my sojourn in New York came to an end, I returned to the UK. As part of my continuing wish to understand myself better, I started spending time with a group that organized retreats based on a mix of psychology and spirituality. Over the next few years, both as a participant and a volunteer, I witnessed hundreds of people tell their stories of suffering. While each testimony had its own individual mark, I came to realize that when I looked below the surface, I glimpsed a common story.

We sometimes like to make our lives very complex, but at the core, what we want is so profoundly simple: to be loved, to be seen, to be recognized, and to feel there is a meaning to our lives.

I slowly developed confidence in my own life by ceasing to search for love outside of myself and beginning to appreciate my inner qualities, recognizing that they had matured in me because of all the pain I had endured, not in spite of it. Over time, I started to like myself; I could smile into the mirror and see myself smiling back with compassion and tenderness glinting in my eyes. I reached the point where I was able to say I loved myself. I felt I had broken the code, had opened the door to my own prison. My life changed on a dime: I went from wanting to extract love from others to wanting to give it. After accustoming myself to a bowl that felt eternally empty, I now had a bowl that was overflowing.

It was a few years later that I came into contact, via my wife, Paz, with Thay and Plum Village. The practices I've since learned have given me the fuel to take the next steps on my journey and to uncover deeper levels of belonging and stability. On my first visit to the Plum Village practice center and monastery in France, Thay agreed that my wife and I could be married in the main meditation hall. The day after the ceremony, he honored us with an invitation to tea.

I remember so clearly entering his room with my wife and seeing Thay sitting with his back to us, swaying gently in a hammock. Two monastic attendants sat on the ground next to him. The tableau felt ageless. Thay got up, and we sat together in a small circle. In similar fashion to my initial conversation with my therapist in New York, Thay began with the simplest of questions: Had I enjoyed my stay in the monastery? I surprised myself by sharing that these had been the two happiest weeks of my life. When he inquired further, I said it was the first time in my life that I had truly touched peace and felt at home. Being within the milieu of mindfulness and in the embrace of a compassionate intentional community, I had felt safe enough to take off the suit of armor I normally had strapped around my body and just be present. The wish I had made in New York—to find a moment of true peace—had been fulfilled.

Coming Back to Life

A few years ago, an organization I work with invited me to help facilitate the first interdisciplinary convening of experts from around the world on the issue of civilizational collapse. During the four-day retreat in Denmark, I did an exercise with the acclaimed philosopher and activist Bayo Akomolafe. We each wrote our deepest desire on a piece of paper and then walked down to the sea, stood in the shallows, and shared our aspirations.

I had written nine simple words: *I want to come home to my true self.* As I read them aloud, I felt a moment of deep disappointment—I was still asking the same question I had first asked many years earlier. But then I experienced something close to an epiphany. I had the insight that a wish to expand my question lay underneath this frustration. I had been taking too narrow a view by wanting to come home to myself, I realized—at the core was my mistaken view of the nature of existence.

As I stood looking into the depths of Akomolafe's eyes, feeling connected in a way that was beyond space and time, I tore the page into tiny pieces and threw them up into the air. As I did so, I told him; "I don't just want to come back to my true self, *I want to come back to life.*" I watched the wind blow the bits of paper about. Some landed in the Atlantic Ocean, some on shore, and some on Akomolafe's tunic.

It was a perfect metaphor: I am much more than myself alone, and to return only to myself would be to miss the core wisdom of "no-self" Thay so eloquently teaches. I am part of the world and the world is part of me; there is nothing that is not me, and I am in everything. The resonance of interbeing I felt standing on that beach wasn't just an intellectual understanding of the nature of interdependence. Though it soon slipped out of reach, that experience—fleeting and joyous—is like a north star always shining and pointing out the way. There are moments when it illuminates my life and then, just as quickly, it disappears behind clouds. Yet I know the insight remains.

The Dark Shoreline

In 2024 I experienced the unpeeling of another layer in this long journey of seeking calm in the storm. The feeling of sitting at the edge of my own ocean of suffering that I had experienced as a child had evolved over time. This ocean, I had come to recognize, contained not just my sadness, but the suffering of the world—much like an empath can experience the collective pain of humanity. A friend helpfully pointed out that in mythology, the ocean represents the vast individual and collective unconscious.

I set myself the challenge of learning the art of sitting on that dark shoreline. Much like the siren calls attracted sailors to their doom in ancient Greek myth, the deep waters pulled me toward them. My lesson became learning how to neither drown in nor turn away from the enormity of this ocean of suffering. I remembered writing an article in *The Guardian* back in 2014 in which I asked a question that had long been on my mind: Is it possible to hold all the grief in the world and not get crushed by it?

Then one day, as I was gearing up to write this book, a vision came to me while I sat in meditation. Suddenly, I recognized that it no longer served me to sit next to this ocean; at the same time, I experienced fear at the prospect of leaving everyone else behind. In my mind's eye, I saw myself getting up from where I was sitting, and I felt a leather strap around my forehead that was attached to a giant net that lay along the entire bottom of the ocean. As I tried to walk away, I attempted to drag all of humanity with me—obviously an impossible feat. At that moment, I saw another way. I removed the leather strap and just started walking away. Eventually I came to the shade of a tree and sat down to rest.

A deep desire arose in me to remain seated here in this place of peace, joy and serenity and offer this as a refuge to others who wanted to sit here with me. It brought to mind an insight I gained many years ago that my path in life is to take people's pain, burn it in a furnace, and transform it into a blessing. I can only hope to do this from a place of being happy within myself.

Maybe the best way to alleviate people's pain is to be truly happy myself; perhaps then my presence would be enough to help those who are now as lost as I was when I was young. In that moment, I felt the innocence of myself as a newborn baby. Like the shepherd in *The Alchemist*, I had found the treasure I had been looking for at the place where I began my journey.

Later that day, I took another look at *The Alchemist* to check the storyline is as I remembered. I smiled when I realized I had forgotten the story ends with the shepherd sitting under a sycamore tree.

An Oracle Reading

Just a few weeks before completing this book, I took part in an oracle reading ceremony at Plum Village to celebrate the Lunar New Year. Decades ago at Plum Village, Thay selected lines from the epic poem *The Tale of Kieu*[8] to arrange into meaningful couplets that people wishing for an oracle reading can randomly choose. Written in the eighteenth century, the poem is so timeless that people have long used it as an oracle to guide important life decisions. The first line of each couplet offers guidance on how to practice, and the second line shares the effect following the path suggested.

I picked an oracle from the hundreds of slips of paper traditionally placed in the main meditation bell, removed it from its colorful embossed red envelope, and read: *All of this time, our hearts have been tied together. Don't stop until you flatten the deep ocean of suffering.* As is customary, I asked one of the senior nuns to interpret it for me. She pointed to the first line—our hearts are tied together—as speaking to happiness and suffering, which cannot exist without each other, in the same way that you cannot separate the left hand side of a piece of paper from the right hand side. We cannot find happiness if we cannot also experience our suffering, and vice versa—they are tied together. If I truly understood this, then I would know the ocean of suffering can exist only if there is also an ocean of happiness. They coexist, the oracle told me; the currents of each flow through the other.

I had spent too long believing I sat at the shoreline of only one ocean.

BREATHER

"Of course you have the right to suffer, but as a practitioner you do not have the right not to practice. We all need to be understood and loved, but the practice is not merely to expect understanding and love, it is to practice understanding and love. Please don't complain when no one seems to love or understand you. Make the effort to understand and love them better. If someone has betrayed you, ask why. If you feel the responsibility lies entirely with them, look more deeply. Perhaps you have watered seeds of betrayal in others. Perhaps you have lived in a way that has encouraged someone to withdraw. We are all co-responsible, and if you hold onto the attitude of blame, the situation will only get worse. If you learn how to water the seed of loyalty in others, it may flower again. Look deeply into the nature of your suffering so you will know what to do and what not to do to restore the relationship. Apply your mindfulness, concentration, and insight, and you will know what nourishes you and what nourishes others."

Thich Nhat Hanh

CHAPTER 3

We Are Not Only Our Stories

There is something cathartic about sharing our stories. It shines a light on our lives. Often, we hide our pain because we believe our feelings will overwhelm us. We worry that, if we let them out, like a genie let out of a bottle, we won't be able to lock our feelings away again if we don't have the strength to face them alone. Feelings of guilt and shame can also make it difficult to share our suffering with others, reinforcing the belief that we are somehow broken or alone in our experience.

In Plum Village, regular sharing circles are one of the most profound communal practices. These facilitated gatherings create space for people to express themselves in a safe way. Retreatants and residents are able to speak vulnerably, knowing that what is spoken is held with compassion, respect, and confidentiality. Those who listen practice deep listening—without judgment, advice, or interruption. In a world where we are often rushed to "fix" things or respond in order not to feel the pain inside ourselves, this kind of silence is radical. It is a great gift for the person sharing to feel truly being heard, seen, and appreciated. It is a great gift to be present for someone who is able to express vulnerability and tenderness. Everyone benefits.

Yet even as we open our hearts, we are reminded: we are not our stories. They are part of us—but they are not the whole of us. Sometimes we hold on to our suffering because it's familiar; our identity has become entangled with the pain, as Brother Phap Huu also shares below. We may sometimes conclude it is easier to maintain the status quo, which we know all too well, even if it means continuing to suffer—we have developed coping mechanisms to deal with what we know. But when stories remain hidden or tightly held, the storm within us can gain unnecessary power. Like a scary shadow cast on the wall by a small mouse walking in front of a lamp, our fear can grow far out of proportion to the truth. With mindfulness and support, we can turn toward this monster of a shadow, see it clearly, and realize that we are greater than what we've experienced.

Some wounds run deep. Sometimes our traumas may be so profound that we cannot summon the strength to face them. But if we are able to find a safe space in which to open up with the necessary support, the benefits over time can be immense. As we have shared in our own stories, this is not about a quick fix or about erasing our past; it is about opening to the slow accumulation of understanding that comes from deeply listening to our own pain. Healing comes from changing our relationship to our stories. From listening with compassion, again and again, until the story no longer defines us, but becomes something we can hold with steadiness. In doing so, we begin to find our footing—not outside the storm, but within it. We discover that even in the midst of uncertainty, imperfection, or anxiety, there can be a calm place to stand.

The Courage to Change

PHAP HUU: Telling our stories is important, but one of the reasons it can be so hard to change is because we're so attached to the story about ourselves—we keep repeating that story over and over and over. We are worried that if we remove that story, we will feel empty and lost. A story can become our comfort blanket, our safety net, a place where we mistakenly believe we feel most secure.

I've heard many people who come to Plum Village share that our way of life is all very beautiful, but that the way we are in the monastery does not work in the real world. They say this to justify not changing. But that's a story. And that story has also been painted by society and maybe also our family, friends, and colleagues. That's why we talk about developing the courage of a warrior to face our own habits and suffering in meditation. This can be very difficult—we need to let go of a layer of who we are, much like a snake shedding its skin. But the beauty of life, something people often forget, is that we're always changing. We can create new stories. The present moment is a paintbrush that you can use to paint and draw a new you. That's the insight of freedom: only the present moment offers you this profound opportunity.

As Thay's attendant, I sometimes heard him say that his ability to be here and sit in the peaceful environment of Plum Village is a miracle. During the Vietnam War, he was almost killed by a grenade on two occasions. He truly understood the meaning of this when he said his ability to be present is a miracle. Thay rarely talked about his past in talks—he did not want people to mistake his use of these stories as asking for love. He only reminded us occasionally of his life in order to wake up those of us living in relative peace and safety while others face bombs, fires, acute hunger, or discrimination.

Thay used these moments to urge us to live deeply, to not waste our lives. I've learned that at the heart of life, the answers are so simple. We just need to start to see that life is very beautiful, and we are very beautiful. With this understanding, we can honor what our stories have taught us, and then we can break free from them.

The Terror of Nothingness

JO CONFINO: In my early thirties, I was on a ten-day self-development retreat in which we spent every day progressively stripping away the layers of our myriad thoughts, perceptions, and beliefs. Individuals were chosen to represent aspects of our minds. On day seven, I was chosen to represent "the terror of nothingness" for the simple reason that I, at that moment, was experiencing that terror—I was recognizing that all my beliefs and perceptions were not the truth but merely a chimera I myself had created in my mind. This insight obliterated the whole superstructure of my life and I did not know at that moment which ground I stood on. During this retreat, the thought frequently arose that if I let go of all my stories, all my beliefs and all my perceptions, nothing would be left of me. From that void, I sensed, the only question to be faced would be the one I had avoided all my life: Who am I?

It was only years later when I was introduced to Thay's teachings that I was ready to see the answer: everything is by nature empty of a separate self. Nothing has an independent existence. Everything is in fact interdependent on everything else. Thay coined the word *interbeing* to illustrate this. I remember arriving for the first time in Plum Village. During lunch, Thay held up a piece of carrot and said that if we looked deeply, we would be able to see the whole cosmos in it. At the time all I could see was the vegetable, but on further reflection, I understood that I would not be able to eat a carrot without the existence of everything else: the soil and the rain, the farmer and the farmers market. A carrot could not exist without the warmth and light of the sun, and for the sun to exist, the whole cosmos needed to be present. From that moment on, I could periodically return to understanding that I cannot be isolated from the rest of life—it takes time to sink in, but the truth is that there is no "I." There is only a vast "we."

We Are Partly Right

JO CONFINO: Whatever story we tell about ourselves, it is important not to rely solely on our own version of events. In our modern era, the disastrous impacts of polarization and the need to be right can be seen only too clearly. As one of Thay's better-known calligraphies asks, *Are You Sure?*

The latest developments in neuroscience support this need to treat our memories with caution. Research shows that the tiny hippocampus organ in our brain, which is just five centimeters long and resembles a seahorse, has an oversized influence on our experience of life. It literally makes up stories, especially when an experience is too traumatic or complex for us to grasp or understand. The hippocampus seeks to simplify our memories, and then we use language to solidify them in our minds.

Even if we truly believe our stories, I always remember Thay encouraging us to see the negative consequences of hanging on to our own version of events. This is particularly the case with those closest to us. If we insist on being right, we have no option but to make our loved ones wrong. They will then suffer, and in turn, so will we. He asked perhaps the most important question: "Would you rather be right or rather be happy?"

It is of great benefit to have an inquiring mind when it comes to the stories we are being told. How often do we meet someone whom an acquaintance or friend may have belittled or criticized, only to find we really like them? Not believing everything we are told is particularly important in these times of mass social media and the continuing rise of fake news. It is increasingly becoming the norm for people to choose what they want to believe based on a narrow view of the world rather than relying on factual evidence, science, or taking the time to listen to their inner knowing.

However aware we may think we are, we each see the world through our own very particular lens and therefore have a built-in bias of which we are often unaware. We live in our own bubble. As a journalist, people often asked me if I was objective in my reporting. I replied by saying it is impossible to be completely unattached—even the order in which I organized a story inherently included some bias. To me, it was more important to understand first of all the purpose behind telling each story, and then to ensure I was being fair, which meant first listening to and then presenting both (or all) sides of a story so readers could open their minds to the nuances and complexity of life rather than relying only on a slim understanding of reality, often magnified by their own echo chamber.

In similar fashion to Phap Huu, I have also learned that at the core, life is extremely simple and yet, at the same time, extremely complex. What is most important is to first understand things at the most profound level and then to add in complexity. It can be much harder to fathom what is most vital if we start off with getting lost in complexity.

Thay taught that it is better to recognize that in any given situation, we are partly right (and therefore partly wrong). My story, for example, that my childhood was dominated by feelings of loneliness doesn't align with my older brother David's memories of me, the youngest sibling, being the center of love and attention. Rather than see these two versions as contradictory, it can be helpful to allow more than one truth. It may be that I was the center of attention *and* I felt lonely. These two versions do not cancel each other out. This way of seeing takes us beyond a binary approach to life. We do not need to choose between happiness and sadness—we can experience both at the same time. They inter-are.

I experienced this for the first time when my mother, in her old age, finally shared with me her experiences of being a fifteen-year-old leaving Germany alone after the

Gestapo ransacked her family apartment during Kristallnacht. She described waving goodbye to her father from the train platform, and in my mind, I could only imagine that she felt unimaginable pain at that moment. I had no bandwidth to imagine any other scenario. She shared that it was emotionally wrenching to leave her father but then added that she also felt a great excitement—she was going on an adventure. I remember so clearly the shock I felt when I realized she had experienced a moment I could only see in one dimension in an entirely different way—she had felt both joy and deep sadness.

This understanding has taken time to ripen in my mind. What helped deepen this insight, was an event I attended in New York with an American-born right-wing rabbi living on Israel's West Bank and a Palestinian activist living in a neighboring community. The rabbi started the conversation by sharing that he believed God had instructed him to come to Israel; he did not consider the land he lived on to be the West Bank, but the Biblical Jewish homeland of Judea and Samaria. He then said he hadn't had any close contact with Palestinians, whose communities were separated from him by fences and mutual distrust. Then the rabbi shared how one day he met the Palestinian activist, who repeated exactly what he himself had been saying about his own life: this land on which he lived had been God given, and he carried out God's work by living there.

At that moment, the Rabbi had a deep realization. It's not that he suddenly changed his view about the purpose of his life and God's message to him, but he recognized that the Palestinian activist also experienced his life with equal belief and passion. He said: "I recognized that there is more than one truth. I learned that I need to incorporate not one truth, but two truths." With that insight, the two started to work together on the slow and painstakingly difficult journey of encouraging two peoples to share the land they both care deeply about.

How We Hold Our Stories

JO CONFINO: When I work as a coach, reframing the way someone is looking at their lives—changing their worldview—is very useful to help people lessen the weight of the baggage they carry as a result of their life stories. I first learned this in my thirties, when a mentor of mine gently suggested that for many of us, our greatest gift is hidden underneath our greatest pain. He explained that our ego uses our suffering in a perverse way to protect us from living to our fullest potential, of which we often don't feel worthy, due to fear.

When I reflected on this, I realized my deepest fear was to be humiliated. My experience of humiliation had been so intense in my early childhood that I never wanted to repeat it. The way to keep safe was to stay hidden away, almost invisible, so this painful feeling did not have a chance to break through my defenses and burst into the open.

But I didn't know at the time that we cannot shut off one emotion in isolation; if we close down our feelings of pain, we cannot help but also cut off our feelings of joy. So, the result of creating this protective shield had been to see home as a small and isolated place. While being invisible helped me avoid feeling shame, it also contributed to my feelings of loneliness and of being an outsider.

Working with my mentor, I decided to upend my old belief and to see that my fear of humiliation was blocking another, more positive attribute: courage. I recognized that because I already knew what humiliation felt like, it could not actually hurt me more than it already had. Like an inoculation against diseases, I already had the antibodies inside to deal with this pain, should it arise again. This new understanding allowed me to reframe my place in life. Rather than feel afraid, I could step forward, take risks, and dance on the edge. The worst that could happen was that I would reexperience an old feeling, one I am now better equipped to deal with.

When clients now tell me their deepest fears, I ask them what secret payoff they think they gain from this belief. Their response has universally been that their fear is a protective cloak. Once they recognize this and see that this way of showing up no longer serves them as adults, they are able to start reframing their experience.

They see that our early childhood experiences can be transformed in our minds to become a source of strength rather than of weakness.

BREATHER

"At times we suffer so much we want to run away. We feel burned out, overwhelmed, and so we take refuge in our projects, even our projects for social change. At these times we need a source of peace and joy, but when we arrive home, we may find a lot of violence and suffering there.

We begin to practice mindful breathing, and after a while, we are able to touch real peace and joy. Going home and touching peace is a source of great nourishment. The practice is to arrive home in each moment, to touch the peace and joy that are within us, and to open our eyes to the wonders of life around us—the blue sky, the sunset, the eyes of our beloved. When we do this, we experience real happiness. When our mindfulness has become strong enough, we can touch the war that is also going on inside us. But we must be careful. If we touch the suffering too soon, before we have developed concentration, stability, and the energy of mindfulness, we may be overwhelmed."

Thich Nhat Hanh, 1994

CHAPTER 4

The Calm

After walking through our suffering, naming the patterns that pull us away, and gently loosening their grip with insight and compassion, we turn toward the experience of returning to stability. This part of the journey isn't about arriving at a fixed destination; it's about rediscovering that we never truly left—we simply forgot how to be with ourselves. Coming home and cultivating calm in the storm means learning to rest again in the simple, sacred rhythm of the present moment.

In this chapter, we offer personal stories as well as concrete practices that have helped us and many others cultivate stability and clarity amidst the turbulence of modern life. These are not lofty ideals or abstract philosophies; they are rooted in the body, grounded in the breath, and available in each step we take. Mindfulness, meditation, conscious breathing, and skillful use of technology are all ways we can reconnect with our center—our true home.

There is no perfect way to return, no correct posture or number of minutes required. The invitation is simply to begin again, as many times as needed. Whether you are walking down a crowded street, answering a difficult email, or watching the sky shift colors at dusk, each moment offers the chance to touch peace, to cultivate stability again. Let these practices be companions—not obligations—as you continue along the path of presence.

Be Beautiful, Be Yourself

JO CONFINO: Thay has a wonderful calligraphy: *Be beautiful, be yourself*. One of the biggest mistakes we can make is to believe we are ugly, either in body or in mind, and therefore to move away from our center, to pretend to be someone else to be considered beautiful. So many people suffer from imposter syndrome or a fraud complex. People do not feel they are good enough as they are and therefore put themselves under great pressure to be a different version of themselves, a version they hope will make them more palatable to others.

Many people use the phrase "Fake it till you make it," which is another way of saying "I have to pretend I am better than I am to survive in this high-pressure world." Wouldn't it be better to reframe our situation in a more positive way? "I accept where I am and commit to learning as I go along. I trust that I have the inner capacity to grow and develop." This is not just a positive affirmation, but the truth—it does not have a final destination in mind, but helps develop trust in each step of the journey.

It's very easy to get lost when we are untethered. If we start off with the belief that we are not good enough as we are, we are actually telling ourselves a story, and we often come to believe what we are telling ourselves. The risk is that however skillful we become, we continue to believe we are not good enough.

I've known many leaders of large organizations who still fear being "found out," even though they are at the so-called pinnacle of their career. Many years ago, I chaired an international sustainability conference where the CEOs of two of the world's biggest companies, IKEA and Unilever, were the first two speakers. The head of Unilever, then considered the leader in the field of business and sustainability, was on the schedule to speak first, with the CEO of IKEA, who was fairly new to the position, immediately following him. The IKEA team approached me and asked for the order to be switched—the IKEA boss was worried he would be overshadowed by his peer if he went second. I, of course, agreed; I knew how he was feeling, and I had compassion for him. He may be the leader of a global business, but he is also a vulnerable human being like the rest of us.

Looking deeply, we can see it is hard to gain true insights from a place of uncertainty when we don't feel stable in ourselves. Like a farmer who imagines the soil of his land is rich with nutrients and then cannot understand why their seeds do not grow into strong plants, we may be puzzled when we lack confidence in our abilities. If the truth is that the fields are full of stones and the soil is badly degraded, it's better to accept that fact and work to clear the land and enrich the soil. We need to face the sources of our anxieties and do the loving work to see ourselves clearly. That is the only way to bring true stability.

I see this pressure to perform in all areas of society—even in Plum Village! Some young monastics want to be perfect monks and nuns; they want to be more advanced in their practice than maybe they currently are. While that can be a commendable aspiration, it can also be a trap. One young monk recently came to visit our house for tea. The two of us sat together at the top of our garden, which has an expansive view over the countryside toward Plum Village. He shared from the heart that he was suffering because he did not feel he was advancing quickly enough; he was doubting his practice. I asked him to stand up and I pointed to the rectangular garden table nearby. "Imagine the width of the table represents your journey through life," I said, "with the left side representing struggle and suffering and the other end representing peace and deep understanding. Now stand in the position where you feel you honestly are." He moved to the far left hand end of the table. I then asked him to keep his left leg where it was and place his right leg at the spot along the table where he was pretending to be. He took a big step to the right; his legs were now quite far apart. I gently pushed him, and he collapsed to the ground—in that stance, he had no stability.

He got the message, and we then talked about how the perfect place for him to be was in his suffering, where he had a real chance to work with it and transform it. That would be closer to being a perfect monk—his aspiration was to help other people find a path through their pain, so it was imperative he first take that journey himself.

It was a powerful physical representation of the situation so many of us are in. We can grow only from the place we currently are. That is our center at that moment, so it's better to call it by its true name and to see it from a place of compassion rather than judgement. We can say with honor that we are imperfect and we have a lot to learn, that we experience fear and anxiety, make mistakes, are sometimes naive and sometimes feel frustrated and angry by how we respond to life. It's more than okay—it's what's called being a human being.

Practicing Compassion

PHAP HUU: In each and every one of us is a beautiful seed of compassion. To cultivate this seed, we need to have understanding. To understand, we first learn to listen. Before we can listen to someone else, it is important to listen to ourselves. When we listen inwardly, we may recognize that there is some pain, some suffering, some fear inside of us. We learn to be present for these feelings, to recognize them and embrace them.

By practicing like this, we don't become afraid of ourselves. We don't push our suffering away, but we first of all recognize it. We can transform it in this very moment by calling our suffering by its name. *Hello my suffering. I know you are here, but I am also here for you.* If we cannot embrace it on our own, we can open our hearts and let in the collective energy of mindfulness.

We can also understand that when we embrace our pain, we do so not just for our own benefit—we also embrace it for others. As we listen and breathe mindfully, we open to what is manifesting in us in this very moment. We do this with the insight of interbeing, recognizing that our whole ancestral lineage and all of society is also present in us. As we practice compassion, we also practice compassion for our loved ones. There may be someone who is very dear to us, who we know needs our love. We can visualize them in this very moment and send the energy of peace.

Then we can also send this energy of compassion to the world. That does not mean only to humans, but to all of the other beings that coexist with us. We aspire in this moment to protect and to care for this planet together. This is a very beautiful way of meditating on love and compassion.

Reclaiming Our Innocence

JO CONFINO: There is something very powerful about recognizing our innocence. Many people I coach suffer from guilt, whether from a religious upbringing or as a result of not forgiving themselves for events that took place in the past. Guilt is like a heavy backpack we carry with us all our days—it literally weighs us down and drains the joy from our lives.

I can recount situations in my life that I still look back on with regret, things I did for which I'm not sure if I will ever completely forgive myself. I occasionally feel pain on remembering them as though these experiences are like scars on my body. But I have also learned to see the essential innocence inside of myself and others and to recognize the positive intentions we have within us. This can lessen the load on our backs.

I once had a powerful experience of reclaiming my innocence. While being guided through a visualization, I remember standing on the edge of an abyss and having the courage to leap into the unknown. I fell into the dark void and floated down until I eventually landed safely at the bottom. I saw a dimly lit path and followed it until I reached a huge cavern in the rocks, where I saw a still lake of water. A bassinet with a baby inside sat on the far side of the lake. I walked around the lake to the small child and picked him up. Looking into his eyes, I saw his innocence. I hugged the child close to my heart, and as I did so, I had the sudden realization that I held myself as a baby. At that moment, I felt myself suddenly transported to the surface of the earth and into a bucolic spring day in the countryside. The sun shone on a meadow full of wild flowers. Undulating hills rolled into the distance. I had reclaimed my innocence.

Being Alone Without Being Lonely

PHAP HUU: Recently I've been allowing myself to have more time alone, time when I'm not formally meditating but when nobody can ask me a question or bother me—time to just breathe, to read, or to listen to something. This solitude is important for me so I can be energized and engaged with my community, whether I'm offering a class, facilitating a meeting, or simply having a cup of tea with someone.

The language of love includes care for myself. Self-care is not spiritual bypassing. Identifying when I need time to tune in to my own needs and cut off the winds of the world helps my consciousness be not always stimulated by outer phenomena. Thay once said that we have the equivalent of many doors and windows: our eyes, our ears, our nose, our tongue, our taste, and our mind. If they are open all the time, it impacts our state of being. Mindfulness practitioners learn to intentionally close these windows and doors. This helps make sure that any emotional storm that arises can settle so we can allow ourselves to feel what is present and what needs tidying up.

We can also give ourselves space by finding time to share deeply with others. Once a month in Plum Village, we monks practice Beginning Anew, a session in which we listen deeply to one another and express our regrets and aspirations. During this time, we share where we're at in the present moment in our practice. One brother, a fellow monk, acknowledged recently that he's been very agitated and that his reactions have been growing sharper and stronger. He shared that he suffered a soft burnout at the end of our busy summer retreat schedule, a month-long period during which we open our doors to thousands of visitors. In acknowledging, seeing, feeling, and speaking to this, he created a bit more space for himself. That is already love.[10]

Don't Be Overwhelmed by Your Emotions

PHAP HUU: I remember Thay giving a teaching in one of the Plum Village summer family retreats I attended as a teenager. He reminded us teenagers that the art of mindful breathing can sometimes be a lifesaver. He asked all the teenagers to put their hands on their bellies and just feel the rising and falling of our breath. He asked us to ground all our thinking and all our feelings and emotions in the rising and falling of our tummies and in this moment to remind ourselves that we're alive. Right here, right now. We are a part of this earth. We are a continuation of our loved ones, our parents, our ancestors. We are a continuation of our friends. Our loved ones are present within us.

With each breath, we stay connected to the rising and falling of our stomach. From this place of stability, Thay invited us to share with ourselves that any emotion—despair, worthlessness, pain—is impermanent. It comes and it will go. Everything that arises is subject to fall. Our pain, our sadness are of the nature of impermanence. All the while, he reminded us to continue to breathe deeply in and out, feeling our breath through the rising and falling of our abdomens. We know that even a great storm will come to an end.

When Thay finished the exercise, he said, "So, young people, remember: do not die because of one emotion. Do not die because of one feeling. We are much more than just that one feeling and that one emotion. We are all the potentials that have been given to us, we are all that we have received. Even if in this moment when there is pain, there is suffering, we are much more than that."

JO CONFINO: This teaching is so important, especially as young people are especially vulnerable to taking their own lives from deep despair. They often hit this point when they are overwhelmed by their emotions, by anxiety, and in that moment see no hope, no way out.

I wish I had met Thay and been able to understand the importance of breathing into our pain when I was a teenager. I did not view my breath as being a place of refuge—I was hardly aware I was even breathing. I remember attending a weekend workshop in my early thirties: at one point the lead facilitator asked people to raise their hand if they'd ever had a death wish, if there had ever been moments when they just wanted to quit life. I put my hand up, and I remember being surprised by how many others also raised their hands. It brought home to me how many people have these moments when it's all too much and it feels like taking our lives is the only way to touch peace. Seeing how many other people knew this deep desperation brought up forgotten memories, which I had repressed until that moment, of driving in my car and thinking of just not taking the next curve—going off the road instead, crashing and ending it all.

I have come to recognize that the most difficult moments of our lives are often a gateway to a new way of seeing and experiencing ourselves and the world. If we had not experienced that level of pain, we may not have been jolted out of our habitual way of thinking. Someone once shared a Korean proverb with me: if the sky were to fall on you, there will be a hole through which you can escape. This has always stayed with me; it has come to my aid during moments of my deepest pain—there is always a way through, though sometimes we need patience to see it.

I have also learned to recognize that when we really feel calm and stable, we can start to accept our pain and the scars of our lives. When we're in this space, we can truly be present for the suffering of others. Often, people who are fearful of their own emotions will seek to close down others' pain—it is too much for them to bear. We are like tuning forks; if someone is resonating to a particular vibration, it causes an identical one to start "singing" in us. In these situations, that person will often tell the one who is suffering to put the past behind them, to get on with their lives, or not to take the particular issue so seriously. This repression may work in the short term, but the pain will find a way to reassert itself—sometimes with even more power and fury.

When someone is locked inside their own hell, the best option as their friend or as a coach is not to try to convince them of how wonderful they are; first, simply have the capacity to sit with them in this dark place, to breathe with them so they can know they are not alone. If we are able to sit together and feel peace in ourselves, the resonance of our tuning fork can help the other person reawaken their capacity for self-care and self-illumination.

In the film *When Dreams May Come*, the lead character played by Robin Williams goes to hell to save his wife, who had committed suicide over her inability to deal with the deaths of her children. He is told he is only able to be with her for a short while or risk himself being trapped in hell. When his time comes and he has been unable to reawaken her, he commits to staying with her. It is only in this moment of unconditional love that his wife wakes up to her situation and they are both able to find a way out.

My first understanding of what it means to be fully present for another person came in a workshop during which a dear friend shared that he saw no purpose in continuing his life and felt suicidal. I felt shocked. I stood up and showered him with affirmations of all the positive qualities I knew were within him. But my love and support were misplaced; he was not in a place where he could receive my praise. The group facilitator looked at me before pointing out that telling someone who is feeling worthless how wonderful they are can drive them further into their loneliness—better to just be fully with them in their pain and to feel the resonance of my own suffering.

Developing our own capacity for healing is in service not only to ourselves, but to all the people we meet. The extent to which we trust in our own abilities is the extent to which someone else will place their trust in us. If we show up fully in our joy *and* in our pain, we give permission to others to do likewise. If we stay closed down and fearful when we encounter unpleasant or frightening emotions, we should not expect anything different from those around us.

I coach a number of senior leaders engaged in systems change who are working hard to convince citizens around the world to wake up and change the way they live, in service to creating a more sustainable and regenerative world, But more often than not, these leaders find it difficult to change their own behaviors. When I point this out to them, it's like a light bulb turning on in their heads. If they're unable to shift, then how can they expect others to do the same?

PHAP HUU: Some people suffer so much that they don't want to be here anymore. They feel like removing themselves from this planet so they can end all suffering. I recently lost a very dear friend who took his own life. I later learned he had bipolar and deep depression. At the moment of his passing, he was alone, without much community or many friends around him. This feeling of separateness in our modern way of life can be so strong. It can be so hard to feel supported. Even if support is available, it's sometimes hard to ask for help when we feel so helpless. It's a dark tunnel when someone goes through this, and I wish I could have known what he was going through before it was too late.

If I had been aware of his situation, my message to him would have been: *Your pain is not yours alone and, although it can come across as a little bit selfish, your life is not yours alone, either. If you die, we are all affected.* There's a part of me that died with him. There's a part of me that returned to the earth with him. I'm still grieving his passing; he helped me through some of my deepest crises. Now, as someone who is still alive, I can say that so many of my actions are for him. I am inspired to be his continuation—all the help he's given me nurtures my aspiration to help others. *Your death is not yours alone. It is all of our deaths also.*

Do You Want to Be Happy or Be Number One?

JO CONFINO: Thay talked a lot about not wanting to be number one in life. He taught that wanting to be number one implied not being able to experience happiness until you reached that position as well as living in fear of falling from that pedestal even if you do ever reach it. He once asked the billionaire CEO of a California technology corporation if he wanted to be number one or to be happy. The business leader said he wanted to be both—Thay cautioned him that he would need to choose one or the other.

If we are to make a choice, wouldn't we really want to choose our happiness? In principle, perhaps, but often there is a pull to make decisions that will help us buttress our sense of self and look good in the world, even if we have to sacrifice our happiness. I vividly remember when Thay spoke to lawmakers at the Houses of Parliament in London. One of the politicians shared that British politics is based on an adversarial system, where MPs sit opposite each other and constantly challenge each other, seeking to prove their way is right. He asked Thay about his view of this model of governing. Thay thought for a few moments, and then asked: "Does it make you happy?" It was so outside of what the parliamentarian expected that he didn't know how to respond. Thay's question, so simple and yet so profound, is something we could all benefit from regularly contemplating ourselves.

There were two such key crossroads moments in my own career. In both of them, I chose jobs I felt would give me greater happiness rather than falling into the trap of taking positions that would impress people. Making those choices, however, was not easy—the voice demanding I prioritize status was loud and alluring, and the voice suggesting I choose happiness was gentle and no louder than a whisper.

The first crossroads came in my early thirties when I returned to the UK from my posting in New York as Wall Street correspondent for *The Daily Telegraph*. I had been offered two jobs: a high-paying, high-status position on a mass market tabloid national newspaper as the head of foreign news as well as the business and finance departments, and a position as the deputy news editor of the business and finance section of *The Guardian*—a position that looked at best like a sideways step and at worst a step down. There was a lot of pressure on me to take the higher-status job, which would help elevate my career, but I chose *The Guardian* post. I could see the other job was a chimera; it was the career equivalent of fool's gold, shiny to look at but not the real thing.

The second crossroads came at a point when I found it difficult to choose between two jobs. I approached the person who had trained me as a coach for support. He recommended me to the person who had trained him, and we met, of all places, in a small café in the arrivals lounge of Gatwick Airport. I explained my situation. I remember only one thing he said, which reverberated in my mind: know the difference between what I was good at and what I loved.

He said the majority of people take jobs because they have developed a particular skill; when a post is offered to them, they think they have the relevant expertise to carry out the tasks, so they are pulled to accepting the job. They take the safe option because they have a narrow view of success: carrying out what they are already accustomed to doing. Fewer people take a job outside of their comfort zone even if they feel in their heart that they would love it. Of course, these considerations apply to any number of decisions we might have to make as we navigate our lives. The common denominator is the recognition that you are shaping your own path and taking the time and space to decide based on your own vision for your life.

The Zen Sword

JO CONFINO: I attended a weekend workshop many years ago where one of the participants came to address his gambling addiction. He needed quite a bit of attention, and the facilitator gave him plenty of space and time to process the roots of his addiction while helping him to understand how he could empower himself to take another approach.

On the last morning, as the facilitator was weaving together the threads of our collective experience, the man interrupted to ask for yet more advice—he was worried that when he left, he would go straight back to gambling.

The facilitator turned to the man and said, "Just stop." It was brutal, in a way, but it also felt like the facilitator cut through the man's fears with a Zen sword to point out that, at the end of the day, the man had to make the choice himself.

I had a similar experience with a mentee who was going round in circles complaining about how she was incessantly judging herself and, as a result, finding it difficult to make decisions about her life and engaging in some unhealthy habits. After we explored this territory for some time and understood the core of her patterns more deeply, I sensed that we could go on forever in the same cycle unless she started to take action. We came up with a practical plan that relied on her connecting to her inner strength to put into effect. It was a reminder that we can tie ourselves in knots when we talk ourselves into paralysis.

In the Ancient Greek legend of the Gordian Knot, there is an oracle in the city of Gordium, now part of Turkey, who says that anyone who could untie a series of elaborate knots tied to an ox cart would rule over all of Asia. When Alexander the Great entered the city, he spent some time trying to untie the knots, but when that was unsuccessful, in one fell swoop he cut through it with his sword.

The Practice of Loving Ourselves

PHAP HUU: Love is a very beautiful word, but the definition of love has been narrowed. It leans toward lust, desire, and romance. But the word love in Zen is very deep, and there are so many layers to it. Love always starts with oneself. Can we learn to be kinder? This is a real practice.

I recently overheard a conversation between a Western monastic Dharma teacher and a Vietnamese nun. The cultural differences were very apparent. The monk asked the sister how it was possible for her to move in the world with such grace while other people carried around such a heavy energy. The Vietnamese sister said, "Well, it's because I know how to love myself." The Western brother replied that he found it difficult to truly love himself, to which the sister responded: "It's so simple. You just learn to care for yourself. You just learn to smile to your suffering. You just learn to accept yourself." I heard the Western brother say, "That's exactly what I can't do."

The brother then turned to me and asked me if I love myself. I replied that I can and I do. I told him I had learned to prioritize my well-being after realizing during my decades of living in a community that knowing how to care for yourself is absolutely essential. When you know how to care for yourself, you care for the collective. Rather than relying on others, you can be responsible for your emotions and feelings.

Knowing one of the causes of our suffering is not knowing how to love ourselves, we can use the art of meditation to look deeper. Why is it that we can't love ourselves? What makes it so difficult to say the word "love"? We can be careful not to limit our understanding of love—acceptance is love. When I am overwhelmed, for example, I know how to pause and go for a walk in the forest. I give myself these moments of relaxation. That's learning to love myself.

When I say I know how to love myself, it's not like I'm patting myself on the back and saying, "Phap Huu, well done, you're an amazing person." Actually, that kind of self-praise is very egoistical in Vietnamese culture. I couldn't bring myself to say that. When I speak to my mother, I can't say, "I love you, mom." Culturally, it would be a very hard thing for me to say. But I can share how much I care for her by checking in on her health, asking about her happiness, and making sure she is eating well. That's our love language in Vietnamese. We can expand our definition of love.

At the beginning, of course, we need some guidance, but we need to pick ourselves up and be responsible for our own learning. We have to tap into the insights already inside of us. What is critical is that we don't give up when it comes to transforming our minds. For example, meditation is a journey where the destination is in every moment. The destination isn't about being able to sit without moving while having no feelings. The aim of meditation is not to erase all feelings, emotions, and thoughts. It's learning to ground ourselves; it's learning to guide our energies and to cultivate our mind. It's cultivating stability and calm in the storm, no matter our anxieties.

JO CONFINO: It took considerable time for me to be able to love myself and even now, when I hit a tough patch, old feelings of self-doubt can reemerge. From the moment I was able to love myself, my life opened up—I became gentler, more generous, more compassionate, and more accepting. For some people this may be a quick process, but for me it took considerable time. It was akin to building a house: creating a foundation that could support a structure and then adding one brick at a time. For quite a while it looked like nothing was happening and then all of a sudden, I reached an invisible tipping point and could see my home coming into shape.

One of the exercises that helped me, which I sometimes offer to others, is to stand in front of a mirror and look at ourself in the eyes for several minutes. We say that our eyes are the windows to the soul. In my experience, we can forge a deep and tender connection when we look at ourselves and are able to genuinely smile and see the kindness that is there when we start to let go of our negative judgments about ourself.

The first time I did this, I found it hard to face myself in this way, but I did not experience the excruciating pain of a colleague at work to whom I had recommended the exercise. I was supporting him after a cancer diagnosis, and he told me he experienced a high degree of self-hatred. When I suggested he spend time looking at himself in the mirror he responded that he had avoided doing exactly that his whole life unless it was absolutely necessary—even while shaving, he said, he turned away as quickly as possible and did not look himself in the eyes. It took him a couple of weeks to summon up the courage to face himself. When he did so, the first few minutes were agony. When he broke through this barrier, he was surprised to discover he was able to feel compassion and, by the half-hour mark, even love. It was a turning point in his recovery.

I have learned from my own experience and through observing many other people take this journey that cultivating self-love is extremely difficult to do on our own. There is a saying that a problem shared is a problem halved. While it is key that we lead, we generally require support, whether from a friend, a coach or therapist, a community, or all of the above. There is something nurturing and healing about being able to voice our fears and heartaches to someone else. When we verbalize our pain, we project our feelings outside of our mind into words and into the world. Beyond the relief of being able to get it out of our system, we are also then able to observe our words with a critical eye. When we voice something, we can be surprised by what we say. That in itself can be a revelation. If we try to do this on our own by observing our own thoughts in our own mind, we often keep going round in circles and it is difficult to know how to intervene. It is similar to a piece of driftwood caught up in an eddy in a river—it keeps going round and round because it does not have the energy to break out into the main flow. Once it does so, it can travel downstream and maybe eventually reach the sea.

Seeing the Good in Ourselves

JO CONFINO: Just as we may find it hard to love ourselves without support, we cannot just tell someone to start loving themselves—often, people do not believe in themselves. I have seen a pattern where we can find it easy to compliment other people, but we often find it difficult to receive praise. We may see this in the way people brush off a tribute or answer an appreciation with, "Oh, it's nothing, don't mention it." I have witnessed people squirm when they receive compliments from a group of people. There is a moment of desperately wanting the acclaim, followed by not being able to take it in and then needing to push it away.

The first time I became aware of this dynamic I was coaching the deputy headmaster of a large public school in London. The man was well-respected, well-liked, and had a job that required tenacity and leadership. I was surprised that in our sessions, he shared only his insecurities. I suggested we name all his positive attributes. I went to a flip chart, marker in hand, and asked him to list his qualities. Silence. After a while, he said he could not think of a single positive thing to say. I suggested he take more time. Still nothing. I took another tack; I asked him to list all the positive qualities his colleagues, pupils, family, and friends had expressed to him. We quickly filled three pages of the flip chart. From this foundation, we were able to find ways for him to start to believe in himself.

If you find it hard to love yourself, try making a list of the good qualities you've heard others say that you have. You can also try making a list of the positive attributes you see in others, and notice that you can only perceive them because those qualities also exist in you.

Belonging

PHAP HUU: If I feel like I want to run away from something, I know I'm not at home in myself. Recently, I've practiced accepting whatever manifests. Whatever happens, there's always a way. It might not be the best solution, but it is the best I can offer right now. I think home, a sense of calm, is not a permanent thing I should be attached to. I am able to feel more at peace in every moment because I know there's no perfect world and no perfect situation. I have learned that home, stability, is in every breath, in every moment during which we are alive. In this way, mindfulness establishes ourselves in our destination: this moment.

When people come to the Plum Village monastery, they often say they feel at home because they are not pulled in so many directions. There's always a storm if you want to see one, but it's possible to be calm within it. The collective space we offer is "just" to be with your breath, "just" to be with your steps, and "just" to walk under the full moon.

I was Thay's attendant, living with him side-by-side, for seventeen years. During these many years, I witnessed that love was always there, gratitude was always there, and of course, mindfulness was always there. When I was with Thay, I always wondered how he was able to generate such a strong feeling of stability, of being at home, when he went through so much pain and suffering during the Vietnam War, was exiled from his homeland for thirty-nine years, and was attacked on a regular basis for his work on renewing Buddhism. Talk about anxiety! But I witnessed that he never allowed that energy to deflect him—he still chose his inner freedom, his way of mindfulness, of insight. He knew what he was doing; he knew his actions were his truest belonging. He left a legacy for the next generation: walking and acting with such freedom, with such strength—being at home anywhere.

JO CONFINO: In my eyes, home is not a singular place or feeling. I can touch a sense of peace and belonging in a place—by the shore of an ocean or sitting under a tree—in another person, a community, or even in my own breath. Home is where I find strength, sustenance, and resilience in both my successes and, when I am able, also in my mistakes. I can accept who I am, how I am, and where I am, and I can feel deeply connected to the people and nature around me.

I feel calmest when I'm able to be fully myself without fear or favor—when I don't have to hide my pain and suffering but can be tender and vulnerable with myself with those around me. On one occasion when my wife Paz and I had tea with Thay, she told him that despite having had the experience of some men treating her inappropriately in other Buddhist spiritual traditions, she felt safe staying in the monks' hamlet in Plum Village as the only woman surrounded by 150 men. Thay responded: "When we feel safe, we feel at home."

I see life as a journey from wholeness back to wholeness. We come into the world as innocent beings and spend our lives looking for ways to come back to this original state of being. In my mind's eye I see the scattered pieces of a 1,000 piece jigsaw puzzle and that our life's work is piecing them all back together. In some mysterious way, it is only through the very pain of fragmentation and the process of healing that we awaken to life's wholeness and develop a deep compassion for all living beings.

Losing our center often happens at an early age. For some of us the reasons are obvious; perhaps we've suffered abuse or neglect. But we can lose our sense of trust from an event as simple as failing to get the present we crave at Christmas—if we believe our happiness depends on it or if we feel unloved if we don't receive it. I recently worked with a coaching client who came to recognize that many of the challenges he faced in life emanated from feeling abandoned the first time his mother handed him over to a stranger at nursery school. It is the only memory he has from his early childhood, and it continues to dominate his way of living: it leads him to avoid making commitments in relationships, to always having an escape plan so he can avoid ever feeling abandoned again.

My wife is an artist, and when we lived in New York, she had an exhibition called "Home as a Shelter." Part of her practice at that time was to weave together discarded objects she found on the street. It's a metaphor for her own healing, collecting lost fragments of herself that she knits back together. This way of seeing has similarities with the core story within my own tradition of Jewish mysticism. The Kabbalah speaks of God filling the entire universe and then withdrawing to give space to creation. The story is that he sent divine light into this primordial space he created to be collected in ten vessels. But the light was so powerful that seven of the vessels shattered and fell into the abyss, which led to the creation of evil. Humanity's task is to help restore these vessels, to bring back the original balance by living a good life.

BREATHER

Farmer and poet Wendell Berry says when he is close to despairing for the state of the world and the future of his children, he goes to "lie down where the wood drake/rests in his beauty on the water . . . [to] come into the peace of wild things who do not grieve their lives with forethought of grief." He takes refuge in the peace of the natural world, and lets go of his anxieties for a moment, to not succumb to overwhelming despair. "For a time," he says, "I rest in the grace of the world, and am free."

Take a moment to close this book and step outdoors if you can. Even if you are in an urban area, you may be able to detect the presence of nature around you, if not in trees and plants, then in the sky above you, the sunlight or moonlight illuminating your vision. Breathe in and out with the energy of mindfulness two or three times and let go of thinking about whatever it is that makes you most anxious, if only for a few seconds. See if you can experience resting in the peace of wild things.

CHAPTER 5

Through Any Storm

We have learned to return to ourselves—to soften the striving, to recognize our worth, and to sit in the quiet shelter of our own presence. From this rooted place, we now begin to look outward—not to escape the world, but to meet it differently. Inner stability is not a final destination, but a foundation.

This is the heart of the practice: not simply to feel calm and stable when conditions are easy, but to carry that calm with us into complexity, into relationship, into anxiety, into the living storm of daily life. When we touch peace within, we become more able to touch suffering around us—not with anxiety and overwhelm, but with clarity and compassion. The perspectives in this section help bridge the inner and the outer, the personal and the collective.

You'll find teachings here that invite you to see more deeply: to reconnect with the earth, to walk more gently, to hold uncertainty with courage, and to act not from fear, but from love. These aren't instructions to "fix" the world, but invitations to show up in it with presence. Just as a tree gives shade by being itself, we, too, can offer stability by staying rooted in what matters most.

Interbeing

PHAP HUU: I think all of us can acknowledge that the notion of a self is a big part of our feeling of separation. In Zen, the ultimate answer is that there is no self—we are made of non-me elements. This is an important notion. Even though we may understand it intellectually, to practice no-self is a life's journey.

It's helpful to begin by deconstructing the belief that we can survive by ourselves alone. Looking into this belief, we see that if suddenly we remove our parents from the picture, we don't exist. If we remove the natural world, we don't exist. If we don't have water to drink or food to eat, we don't exist. If we don't have the sun and the cosmos, we don't exist.

Nothing has an independent existence. Everything is *inter*dependent on everything else. Looking deeply with a calm and wakeful mind, we see in fact nothing has an independent existence. Nothing really disappears; it simply changes. A rose is an example: the beauty and delicateness of a rose is only possible due to *non-rose* elements such as soil, rain, sunlight, and even the gardener as well as their parents and ancestors. All of these non-rose elements *inter-are* with the rose. When the rose dies and can no longer be perceived with our senses, it is transformed into soil. Can you see the rose in the cloud, in the rain, and in the soil?

The cloud does not disappear when it transforms to rain, just as the rain does not cease to exist when the storm stops. The rain is right here in this rose. Rain is in each head of lettuce, and in each human being who eats the lettuce.

This is not merely a concept. It is truly the very nature of existence. Can you look at your enemy with an understanding of interbeing? They are you, and you are them. We all wish for happiness, and we all wish to avoid suffering. We all get stuck, fall down, and misspeak sometimes. Love and compassion allow us to see clearly so we can offer wise understanding rather than blame and judgment.

When we recognize the interdependence of everything, we see more clearly. Our compassion deepens as we understand: I am not separate from you, nor you from me. You are not separate from the sun, the rain, the clouds, or the rose. You are not separate from the earth. As you care for the earth, you care for yourself, for your children and your community. Any solutions—to global warming, species extinction, poverty, conflict, or any other complex issue—requires we diligently practice mindfulness to clearly see our interdependence.

Belonging to a community is very healing in our divided times. Historically speaking, the Industrial

Revolution began to shift our culture and our way of thinking toward individualism and consumption. Over time, we came to believe material possessions could make us feel safe, successful, and at peace.

I remember my first time visiting Vietnam as a child in 2000 and seeing that not everybody had a TV. Growing up in Canada, I assumed every house had a TV. Without one, your house and your life just weren't complete. My first time in Vietnam, I experienced communal TVs—community watching. All the neighbors would gather at the one house in the village with a TV to watch a popular weekly series together. Instead of the owner feeling this was his TV or that he had worked hard for it and only he had the right to watch it, he shared it with everyone.

Community is a vital refuge for all of us who aspire to walk this path of calm in the storm. As an individual, we may have our own commitments and high aspirations, but unless we are very determined, we will likely forget them. Being part of a community can help. We don't have to join a monastery—we can find community everywhere. In community, everyone is a mirror for one other. When I don't feel so good or have low energy, I can take refuge in those around me. My own mindfulness may not be strong enough, but collective energy can help me enhance and nourish my own motivation. I can see another person's smile and be lifted by it. Sometimes just someone's acknowledgment of my presence has an impact.

Often after the holidays at the end of the year, when we may have overindulged, we sign up for a gym membership. We may go to the gym for a few weeks, but then perhaps our old habits kick in. Spirituality is not so different. We may have the wish to be mindful and lead our best life. Mindfulness is sexy now, and many people sign up for mindfulness courses every New Year. That's good, but we have to understand that this practice is not something for a week or a month; like exercise, it's something to bring into our daily lives.

On a daily basis, I practice remembering our community is like a living body. Every member is a cell in this body. There are moments when you have to work at the brain level and place your cell in a leadership position, but at other moments you need to get practical—to cook and offer a really good meal, for example. We dismantle our judgments that we are too important to do more menial jobs, and do everything wholeheartedly. Mindful living is an art.

Reconnecting to Mother Earth

JO CONFINO: As a young child, I was awed by the immensity of the stars shining in the night sky and, on a smaller scale, the life I discovered in the little pond in our local park. In that pond I caught newts and small stickleback fish and watched gatherings of water boatmen insects glide along using their long, oarlike hind legs before suddenly diving below the surface. I often biked across the park through glades of trees and then down through fields before climbing to the top of a bridge and waving to train drivers as they passed underneath.

This love of nature has accompanied me throughout my life; there is nothing I appreciate more than walking the wild cliffs of Cornwall in Southwestern England or hiking in the French and Spanish Pyrenees. But despite all of this, it is also true that I often experience a feeling of disconnection from Mother Earth. I enjoy all her beauty, but I don't feel truly part of her. I feel separate. I can enjoy a beautiful sunset or a majestic forest, but I don't like to walk through bracken or in areas with lots of insects that bite. I am also aware that sometimes I consume nature as a way of maintaining my mental and emotional balance, rather than giving her my unconditional reverence. Like the majority of the world's population, I was brought up in a large city and spent very little time in wilderness areas where I could experience nature in a relatively unadulterated state. Even on my walks in the countryside, not seeing another human being for a whole day feels like no small blessing. Partly because I grew up in the age of scientific materialism, my magical relationship with life was progressively shut down and reduced to facts and figures.

My first recognition of my narrow, human-centric views occurred during my master's degree in business and sustainability, which involved spending a week at Schumacher College, the alternative ecology center in Devon, England. During that time, our group went to an oak forest alongside the River Dart to take part in an exercise. We were split into groups of two and one person was blindfolded while the other supported their partner in navigating the surrounding terrain without harm. Supported by my fellow student and unable to see, I spent the first period of time tentatively feeling my way around, touching the bark of trees, the leaves of plants, the mossy forest floor. We were then instructed to change our way of seeing and to feel nature experiencing us. At the time, this felt revolutionary. I had believed nature is there to be experienced and to meet my needs—never before had I thought that nature is sentient and also feels the impact of our presence.

A series of interviews I did with Thay for *The Guardian* over a period of a few years deepened my understanding of the reasons we feel disconnected from Mother Earth. During our conversations, two things in particular struck me deeply. One was his belief that an underlying anger at being born into a life of suffering is the reason we reap so much destruction on the earth's ecosystems. We know we can sometimes take out our anger over the pain we feel on our mothers, for example, but Thay pointed out that we also take unconscious retribution on our ultimate mother—Mother Earth. When I asked Thay why we are not taking action to halt the loss of ecosystems and countless species on whose life we depend, his most simple of answers resonated deeply: if we do not know how to take care of our own suffering, how on earth can we care for the suffering of the world?

Thay is a poet and rather than translate his words, I want to share a snippet of one of our conversations. These words of wisdom are my go-to place when I need to be reminded to connect more deeply:

> You carry Mother Earth within you. She is not outside of you. Mother Earth is not just your environment. In that insight of inter-being, it is possible to have real communication with the earth, which is the highest form of prayer. In that kind of relationship, you have enough love, strength, and awakening to change your life.
>
> Changing is not just changing the things outside of us. First of all, we need the right view that transcends all notions including of being and non-being, creator and creature, mind and spirit. That kind of insight is crucial for transformation and healing.

> Fear, separation, hate, and anger come from the wrong view that you and the earth are two separate entities, that the earth is only the environment. You are in the center and you want to do something for the earth so you survive. That is a dualistic way of seeing.
>
> To breathe in and be aware of your body and look deeply into it, you realize you are the earth and your consciousness is also the consciousness of the earth.

Thay compares humans to chickens in a cage fighting over the last ears of corn without noticing the butcher has come with his sharp knife. Because of our inability to collapse the gap between human beings and Mother Earth and our myopic view of economic growth, Thay suggests we prepare for the end of civilization. He told me: "For us it is very alarming and urgent, but for Mother Earth, if she suffers, she knows she has the power to heal herself, even if it takes 100 million years. We think our time on earth is only 100 years, which is why we are impatient. The collective karma and ignorance of our race, the collective anger and violence will lead to our destruction, and we have to learn to accept that.

PHAP HUU: In our practice we offer our gratitude to *bodhisattvas*, compassionate beings who work to end suffering. Thay added new bodhisattvas for us to meditate on. One of these is Gaia, Mother Earth. Thay teaches us that we need to fall back in love with Mother Earth so we can hear her cries, see her wounds, and be witness to her suffering—see it as our suffering. Even if we experience despair, we can still see life as beautiful, still see that planet Earth is a miracle. From this place of gratitude, we naturally want to act to protect and help restore degraded ecosystems.

We know we are still alive. Because we are alive, anything is possible. Let us take care of the situation in a more calm and mindful way, rather than acting from frustration, anger, and despair. This is the 2,600-year-old teaching that has been transmitted through so many teachers to our time, and it's still so relevant. It is important to suffer, but from the suffering our insight of understanding and our insight of love can grow.

If all of us can come back and nourish the love inside of us, I believe there is a way to take care of the situation we are in and to offer love back to our precious mother, Mother Earth. With mindfulness, we are in touch with the wonders of life. Most of the time we live in the world, but we are not here. This is why so many of us are attracted to spirituality—without this grounding, you're going to feel so lost and so empty.

JO CONFINO: Whatever our status in society and whatever material possessions we have, deep down inside we are children of this earth. If we lose our connection to our home, to the trees, to the birds, the bamboo, the flowers, how can we say we are alive? To practice mindfulness is to recognize the simplicity of life.

If we are able to be in the present moment, life will present its wonders. Every morning, we recite a *gatha*, or mindfulness verse. The first line is, "Waking up this morning, twenty-four brand new hours are ahead of me." Just that line itself is enlightenment. If you can recognize that you have twenty-four brand new hours, you're not caught in the past, you're not worried about the future. Those twenty-four brand new hours are a gift. With that understanding, your way of living will start to change. That's why gratitude—touching the simple wonders of life, being grateful for your lungs, for the fact that you are breathing, being grateful for the teachers who have helped you to understand, grateful for all the causes and conditions that have brought us to this moment—is so important. We are the environment; the environment is not outside of us. When we experience this, that's enlightenment of the present moment. With this understanding, we keep hope alive.

During a climate leaders' retreat Plum Village held in Canada, there was a moment when all ninety participants sat together. Symbolically seated in the center of the space was an indigenous elder who had fought for many years to stop the destructive extraction of tar sands, a process that emits up to three times more pollution than producing conventional crude oil, depletes and pollutes freshwater resources, and creates giant ponds of toxic waste. The elder shared that a deep-seated anger at the destruction he was witnessing had kept him going all these years, but as a consequence he had become an angry man. He was angry at everyone in his life. It was deeply moving to witness the fullness of his realization that we become what we consume. It was also an important reminder that even in the midst of fear and anxiety, it is important to act from a place of stability and love.

Expressing Generosity

JO CONFINO: One simple way of finding our own center, our calm in any storm, is the counterintuitive practice of reaching out to others with generosity when we ourselves are suffering. When we become obsessed with our own pain, we either tend to isolate ourselves or to strike out at those we believe are responsible for our misfortunes. It can be easy to become victims of our situation.

One of the best pieces of advice I ever got is that when I am feeling low for any particular reason, an effective antidote is to support someone else who is in need. By doing so, we not only help the other person by offering our presence, but we empower ourselves by showing that despite our circumstances, we can water the seed of generosity within us. There are times when we feel down, times when we cannot offer ourselves kindness, but if we are able to offer this to someone else, we will automatically benefit and feel more stable.

There are many ways of expressing generosity—it can be as simple as holding someone in our thoughts and prayers. In this way, we expand our minds and remember there is beauty even among a field of thorns. A more advanced practice, if we have the capacity and inner strength, is to show generosity even to the people we believe are the cause of our suffering. Obviously, this needs to be calibrated to ensure we only act in ways that keep us safe. One of the methods Thay created to help us with this process is to see ourselves as innocent five-year-olds and then to see the people we think of as the cause of our suffering also as innocent five-year-olds. Just a simple practice like this can soften our hearts and help us recognize that we never suffer alone.

Changing the Peg

PHAP HUU: When I visualize going into the future, coming into my late thirties, I don't visualize moving forward as an individual. I bring the insight of how we can walk together to the future. Of course, I want to contribute the best of my capacity as an individual to the great collective. The image that comes to mind is a river. We're all drops of water from different clouds, but we've all come together in this very moment—we're all in this river. If I know how to take refuge in this river, I don't have to hurry to arrive anywhere, and I can learn to enjoy the natural flow of the water. Before I had this insight, I had the idea that I could say I accomplished something when I finished a project. Because of my own role in the community—having the responsibilities of being the abbot and main facilitator at Plum Village—that idea became my way of life. A lot of the time, I was running, chasing after finishing something. I started to see that I was losing myself in that chase, in all that doing, even though it was the most profound work of helping to spread Dharma.

After I finished a project, I may have felt a little bit of happiness, but it left as quickly as it came. I have been able to change this view. The Buddha might say, *Sometimes you are stuck in your view about something because you think it is your happiness. But if you reflect on that view, does it offer you true happiness?* I started to have moments of doubt, moments of just wanting to do nothing. When I looked deeply, I started to see how important it was to enjoy the process and find happiness in it. In the sense that all experience is food for our consciousness, the process as well as the result is also food, a nutrient that gives me insight—I don't have to wait till the end to be fulfilled.

This is what we call "changing the peg." If you know you're doing something that makes you suffer, feel low, or lose yourself, you have to have the courage to change. From time to time, we can get stuck in our aspirations, our ideals, our goals, and fail to see the wonders that manifest when we value the process. When I finally realized the pattern I was stuck in, I opened my blinds a little more, and I saw the gift that is always present. The end is not the happiness. By starting to walk the path, starting to feel my work in this moment as an individual and as a collective, I can see my own growth, my own joy, and my own happiness right here. We can find happiness and success in the very moment we plant the seed of a flower or a tree. If you wait until the seed transforms into a mature plant, you miss the whole miracle of the seed taking root in the soil. You miss the opportunity to connect the seed to the earth, to cultivate it. You miss the experience of love and affection while you care for it and then see it grow.

This has truly given me a lot more energy, a lot more space. I don't just want the gratification of accomplishing something. I still get caught sometimes—when I make progress, I might notice the strength of my habitual thinking and find myself again in that space of "What's next?" and start running again, chasing after future goals. When we speak about aspiration, we also have to look at aspiration with freedom—understanding aspirations aren't always linear.

Remembering You Are Enough

PHAP HUU: During a family retreat at Plum Village, I spent time with a group of teenagers. I asked, "How many of you feel you are not enough?" Eighty percent of them raised their hands. I asked how many of them feel pressured to be someone other than who they are, and nearly everyone's hands went up. How many of them feel lonely? Again, eighty percent.

This snapshot is not so different from what I see in broader Western society. Even as parents, as colleagues, as friends, maybe we unintentionally feed this narrative. We have to be mindful, pause, and take a step back to look at how we live and what we curate in our own minds. What are our views of success, our views of happiness, our views of a healthy life? How are we passing these on to the next generation? It is important we find the courage to change the narrative. This may mean reflecting on our livelihoods, our friendships, the conversations we engage in, and the media we consume.

When we have a new way of seeing, we need the courage to change our habits. That will shift your life. And most of the time, we think, *Oh, the monks can do it because they live full-time in a practice center. I can't because my lifestyle is so different.* But that's a narrative that society has offered you to keep you in line. That's a narrative the advertisement industry is being paid billions of dollars for to make you believe you are not enough, that you need more diplomas, more titles, more money, more fame, more sex, that you need more and more to feel you are enough yet never get to the end of the rainbow.

It can be scary for people when they leave a retreat at Plum Village, which has been a peaceful place for them to slow down and open up. Will peer pressure and the weight of daily life draw them back into their old habits? Will they be able to say no to an invitation to go to a club and suggest instead meeting in a park and having a real conversation? These are some of the things I hear people wonder about when they are preparing to return home. One of our retreatants shared with me that after a retreat in Plum Village, she realized how long it took her to recuperate after just one night out at the bar. She realized the conversation was shallow there, but when she invited her friends to come to a park, only three of them showed up—the rest seemed to feel that wasn't a good time.

When we go back to the world after time on retreat, yes, we will be bombarded by the cacophony of noise in our lives, but our power, our spiritual practice, and our way of seeing and being all offer a reconnection to a deeper part of ourselves. What we can learn from the Zen art of stopping and meditating, reflecting and looking, is that there is actually a different way of really enjoying life: it's much simpler than we think.

Coming to Plum Village or any place once and hoping to completely transform your life is wishful thinking. One retreat can never be enough to change everything in your life, because you need to go home and integrate your transformation in your daily life. A retreat is an opportunity to come back to the calm lake within, where we can feel the coolness that is there and also see a clear reflection, but it takes time to change established patterns of thinking and acting. I continue to listen to some of the most fundamental Zen teachings, and they stay fresh—because I'm still growing. Cultivating stability and calm in the storm is a moment-by-moment opportunity.

Finding Flow in Everyday Life

JO CONFINO: Having a powerful insight into the nature of our lives can feel like a lightning bolt. In one moment, recognition so strong and so clear that it slices through old belief patterns like a hot knife through butter can have a profound impact and create a new foundation for our way of being in the world. The two times I have experienced this have allowed me to see a deeper truth that my egoic and defended mind could not argue against or repel. Insight went to the center of me, and the center of me became illuminated.

But as Brother Phap Huu writes, each illumination is only the start of a journey. Unless we work and develop our insights, they can quickly lose their shining quality and effervescence. It is the same with love. I had a magical start to my relationship with my wife Paz—a true love story. She told me very clearly from the beginning that our relationship needs maintenance, just like a car needs to be serviced for it to continue to run smoothly.

I like the metaphor of a channel of water that has been silted up. To bring back the flow, we need a dredger to come and dig out all the silt, but we cannot then just sit back and think "job done." The process needs to be repeated over time—silt is always flowing down from upstream and will block the flow again if we do not attend to it. This is not so different from how our minds work. We can temporarily clear pain, but it is our habit to suffer—suffering will return. Spiritual teachers are quick to tell us not to become attached to deep spiritual experiences, to hang onto them or seek to recreate them. Better to see the direction they point in, let them go, and keep walking forward.

With every coaching client, I see a common pattern. People get in touch because they know there is something wrong in their lives; it feels at best like a thorn stuck in their skin, irritating them, or at worst like an infected wound causing acute pain. Within a fairly short time, it is usually possible for them to get insight into the root cause of their suffering. It is at this point that clients always respond in the same way: "I now know the cause of my suffering and I want to change, but I don't know how to go about it." This is a pivotal moment. There are two directions the person can take—either they decide the challenge is too great, retreat back into how they were, and make a fresh pact with their pain, or they have the courage to step out of their suffering and then to take another step into the unknown.

We see this choice playing out all around us. We face a climate emergency that threatens the very survival of our civilization and that of countless species. As we get closer to this precipice, we have a choice, whether we consciously know it or not. We can deny there is a problem and retreat back to our old destructive ways or we can truly recognize the scale of the challenge and commit to the radical changes we need to go through to create a more sustainable and regenerative world. We see tendencies to choose the first path all around us: climate denial and renewed support for authoritarian leaders who appear strong but in truth represent our fear. We see backward-facing movements that turn away from an understanding of the power of interconnection, collaboration, and compassion and toward a belief in separateness, protectionism, and hatred.

Thay says when we face difficulty, a wise person asks what they are doing to free themselves from suffering, whereas a foolish person is consumed by how he or she can punish those they believe are responsible. Many people are swayed by the wish to hold on to what they already have, to build a wall around it and to protect it, regardless of the impacts. But others recognize the need to take a courageous stance and trust that a new life is possible, a new life that will create more happiness and equity in the future, even if it is not achievable in their own lifetime. It is like an old person planting an oak tree for future generations. One path is driven by fear, the other by love. We always have a choice.

Don't Run Away

PHAP HUU: There is such strength in being mindful of where our mind goes in moments of hurt. We are so programmed to complain and to judge, to look for the fault outside of us. We think suffering comes from outside, that all the wrong action is nothing to do with me—pain is because of something or someone else. When we think this, we run away from the past and run away from the future. It is important to be responsible for how we handle each situation. When we respond to circumstances with the best capacity we have at that moment, we come home to ourselves, love ourselves, and care for ourselves and the situation.

If we blame others, all we do is tighten the knot of the rope we have tied around ourselves. Everything comes around—if we don't give things the attention they deserve, the problem will come banging on our door, asking for our care, our love, and our transformation. The practice gives us the freedom of choosing how to live in this moment; mindfulness, concentration, and insight give us freedom. Even in the midst of suffering, even in a moment of deep conflict, we still have an opportunity to learn from what is going on. We still have an opportunity to not water the seeds of conflict and to take a step back.

Some conflicts will take time to heal. Maybe you just want things to be the way you want them to be, and you come in and tell the other person how wrong they are and how right you are. Sometimes the best thing to do is to take a step back—to just accept that, for a time, we have a conflict we cannot deal with head on; if we did, we would just clash further. We wouldn't be able to listen to each other, and more hatred would grow. Love is also the ability to know when we don't have capacity. Stepping back is also action.

It is important to question how sure we are of a situation. *Do I have enough understanding, and does the other person have the capacity to handle the situation, or are they feeling overwhelmed? Can we help them grow their capacity?* This is being responsible for the present moment, for this situation. It's very difficult. It asks us to be selfless, but when we're very selfish, our love can be very toxic, our love can be very needy, and we take energy away rather than giving energy. This is deep looking. This is meditation, and insight can grow from it.

Let Go of Attachments

JO CONFINO: Often we get attached to a certain way of doing things or a particular way of thinking. If we get stuck here, we can become brittle and break. But if we are able to look at any situation in a fresh way, we remain supple and are more likely to gain new insights.

I first experienced this working at *The Guardian* while managing a project. The team hit a roadblock; despite all their best endeavors, they could not find a way around it, and they were on the verge of giving up. I asked them to imagine starting the journey again, but this time venturing forth carrying all the experience they had now gained. Starting afresh in this way, would they take the same route, or would another path take them to the place they wanted to go without coming up against that particular roadblock again? They did find another way, and the project continued to fruition.

There are two Zen stories that have helped me to understand the core teachings of nonattachment to particular outcomes. The first tells the tale of two monks about to wade across a river. One of the monks notices a beautiful young woman who's hesitating at the water's edge. The young woman asks for their help crossing to the other side. The older monk picks her up and carries her across. The other monk is aghast that he touched a woman, contrary to their monastic vows, but doesn't say anything. That evening, the younger monk confronts the other monastic and asks why he broke his precepts by carrying her across. The other monk replies, "I let her go as soon as I got to the other side, but you are still carrying her." It is a great illustration of how important it is to not be attached to the past—it infects our whole system, and we can become obsessed with our own views about how we think things should be.

The second Zen story points out that even when we want to let go of our attachments, it can be extremely difficult. In it, a Zen teacher sits with his students and discusses the importance of nonattachment. All of a sudden, a young aspirant runs in and hands the teacher a note. After reading it, the teacher starts to cry uncontrollably. Several minutes later, one of the students plucks up their courage and asks: "Master, why are you crying?" The teacher lifts his head, informs them his son has just been killed in an accident, and carries on weeping. After another considerable period of time, the same student again speaks up: "Why can't you stop weeping? You've just been teaching the importance of nonattachment." Through his tears, the teacher replies, "Some nonattachments are harder and more painful than others."

I remember reading a newspaper article many years ago about a woman who forgave her son's killer. At the time, it shocked me that this was possible, but I remember her explanation: letting go of her anger not only released the killer of his guilt for what he had done but, more importantly, it also released her from a life of bitterness.

In my own life, letting go of my neediness for love and attention has brought me considerable happiness. It took quite some time growing up to see how much of a turnoff my neediness was to others. I imagine most of us have had the experience of being around a needy person. After a while it can feel suffocating, and we just want to get some space. I also see self-sabotage in my old behavior: because I felt unloved, I looked for attention. When I found it, my (at times) overbearing behavior pushed people away, thereby proving to myself that I was indeed unlovable. Examining this habit, I see my story was more important than my happiness. If all of us are carefully attentive to our behaviors, we may see how we reinforce our beliefs at the expense of our happiness.

The most extreme examples I have seen are when people believe their parents have ruined their lives and are fueled by the energy of this rage over many years. Even when their parents are dead, the person continues to unconsciously sabotage their own life—believing the story that their parents are responsible for their failures rather than allowing themselves to have a happy, successful life. If they allowed themselves to be happy, they would have to let go of their laser-focused anger. If you want to get revenge on someone and wish they were dead, build two graves.

Understanding the Mind

JO CONFINO: The Buddhist model of the mind is helpful in understanding why we behave in the way we do. It suggests we have two parts to our consciousness. The first is mind consciousness, the everyday behaviors we can easily recognize. Underneath this is store consciousness, which we are normally not aware of but which contains all the seeds of human experience—from love, peace, and joy to anger, betrayal, and jealousy.

Depending on the circumstances of our lives, any one of these dormant seeds can be watered and rise up into our mind consciousness. The more often a seed has been watered in our lives, the quicker it will respond when it is triggered, and the more likely it will fill every corner of our mind.

Thay used the metaphor of someone coming over for dinner to describe how best to work with our emotions. If the person visiting is being difficult or insensitive, we look for ways to end the evening as quickly as possible. We do not offer coffee and dessert. But if the person is good fun and lifts our spirits, we will seek to keep them at the dinner table as long as possible.

When I'm not included in something, it immediately waters my seed of exclusion. Because I experienced feeling left out so often growing up, the seed immediately bursts into my mind consciousness and triggers any number of emotions, such as anger and jealousy. Because of the power of the feeling, it takes mindful concentration to relax that thought and remind myself this is just the fear I had as a young child showing up again. Conversely, when I was young, I received few compliments, so my seed of self-appreciation doesn't sprout so easily. Now, when someone acknowledges and appreciates me, I no longer brush it off as I used to. Instead, I give myself permission to appreciate the compliment, to welcome it in and ask it to stay a while before letting it go.

Dancing at the Edge

JO CONFINO: Much of the time we get stuck in our beliefs because we grow comfortable with them, even if they cause suffering in our lives. We come to believe *this is just the way we are* and this becomes our comfort zone—we defend our belief, especially if it is challenged, because of our fear of letting go.

Our greatest chance to break through this barrier is to go to our true learning edge. Often, we need support to do so. In my practice as a journalist and a coach, I have learned the value of a good question. I tend to surprise people with my questions, not in order to undermine the people I interact with, but to help shift them away from their pre-planned beliefs and speaking points so they can surprise themselves and find a nugget of gold they had not been consciously aware of. This tends to happen only in the present moment, often when least expected.

I learned this by understanding how change often happens. New innovations tend to develop at the edge of existing systems—mainstream thinking tends to be so dominant, it prevents anything new from emerging. But if something new has the capacity to develop and strengthen, it has a chance to break out and become the new dominant way of doing things.

Not surprisingly, our minds work rather similarly. Our established beliefs and perceptions tend to crowd out new ways of thinking, and so we need to go to the edge of our minds to find the space for new insights to emerge and strengthen. This is a process of constant evolution—what was once at the edge can come into the center, and then something new can form at the edge until, in its own time, it comes to the forefront. This is the nature of impermanence. All systems arise, all systems fall.

I remember being asked to give a talk to a group of Morgan Stanley investment bankers. During the interactive part of the conversation, someone made fun of people who had chosen an alternative lifestyle and lived off-grid. I got quite emotional and challenged the executive to see with different eyes. We should have respect for those people who challenge the existing ways of doing things—they show us another way of living. By protecting their freedom, they also protect our freedoms, even if we ourselves are living a life of conformity.

Beyond Individualism

JO CONFINO: We know one of the deepest reasons for anxiety and feeling we don't belong is because Western society has finessed and spread the belief that we are all separate from each other and that if we do not put ourselves first, we will be left behind or lose what we believe to be ours.

These ideas are reinforced from the day we are born via our education, advertising, and the demands of our working lives. The wilderness areas where we can get outside of our human-centered perspective and touch true peace are being destroyed, making it increasingly difficult to get away from the cacophony of messages enticing us to be more than who we've been led to believe we are. Even our holidays have become drawn into this competitive vortex—people send photos in real time to prove they are having a good time, often exciting feelings of jealousy in the people receiving these images.

We have been living in a world of abundance, but we've been taught to believe in scarcity—that we can be happy only if we accumulate more. Our obsession with materialism has caused us to be obese in our thinking: we always want more, whether it is a bigger house, a more important job, or a more beautiful, sexy partner.

Advertising and media deepen the misperception that we need more by showing us a snowstorm of images of success and beauty, goading us to believe we are not enough and that we need to strive to be like the hordes of social media influencers making money by convincing people they have found the way to happiness. Social media algorithms only drag us further into the mire. *If only I had this, if only I was like him or her, then I would be able to relax; then I will have reached my destination.*

When conditions bring us to question the truth of our individualistic story, whether during our teenage years or in the midst of a midlife crisis, we often find it difficult to break out of this myopic view. Not only have we become addicted to consumerism ourselves, but most of the people around us seem to have bought into the values of the system. Even those determined to live an alternative lifestyle based on non-capitalist ideals find it impossible to completely escape. A close friend who sought to create an intentional community in Portugal, for example, found it difficult for those involved to develop a common vision—he said everyone was committed to living in community, but they each had their own view of what community life was, which they wanted to impose on everyone else!

Reciprocity

JO CONFINO: I am reminded of Thay's saying: *There is no way to happiness, happiness is the way.* Despite the torrent of assurance that the markets will fulfill our need for belonging, a part of us knows true belonging is living a life of reciprocity, giving to our family, friends, and communities from a place of kindness, generosity, and gratitude. A part of us recognizes that when we look after someone else, we are also tending ourselves. If we truly give, we will naturally receive; if we give to get, we are bound to sacrifice and be unable to receive the bounty of our actions.

I am as much a victim of societal brainwashing as anyone else, and I often feel myself being dragged back into old beliefs I know are not true and are not where my happiness lies. At the time of writing this book, I am sixty-three years old. I tell myself I should know better, but I still can feel flames of jealousy arise when I see people I know succeeding—being promoted to a more senior position, speaking at prestigious events, or being fêted and admired.

I find it difficult to even write about this; it brings up embarrassment and shame—these colleagues and friends are people helping to drive positive change in a world on fire. In these moments, it may seem counterintuitive yet it helps me to connect with my many painful childhood experiences of feeling left out, whether that means being picked last for the football team or, as the youngest of six children, watching from the sidelines while my elder brothers worked on car restorations. It's a tender place. When I open the door to it, I am more able to find compassion for myself and to calm my jealous mind. It also helps to remember that I made a clear decision to move the axis of my life from doing to being. When I left my last job as a senior editor in New York, I made a commitment to live next door to Plum Village and *to stop striving after life*. Instead, I decided *to allow life to come to me*, to move from scale to intimacy. In my coaching practice, I never advertise or market what I do—people find me, and I trust in the process.

One inspiration for this change in mindset was an interview I did a few years ago with the most senior Western nun in the Plum Village community. Since she was entering her seventies, I asked after her deepest aspiration for this last period of her life. She replied that she wanted to be the very best person she could be, and that it did not matter whether or not anyone was aware of her actions—her process of purification contributed to the collective consciousness regardless. In a flash I understood that who we are and how we show up are already a contribution to humanity. It was a deep teaching, a reminder not to be caught up only in what we see but to also acknowledge our narrow understanding of consciousness and of our impacts.

What also supports me when I hanker after something else to fill my hole of not-enoughness is to witness the ability of the monks and nuns of Plum Village to touch deep happiness despite having so few material possessions. It is inspiring to see the selfless, communal way they live and serve others. If something goes well, rather than lauding one particular individual, the whole community celebrates.

Once a year during the Lunar New Year, monks and nuns open their private living quarters to visitors, and we get to see their lives up close. The small bedrooms are all shared. Each person has a single bed—often just a wooden board—and very few material goods: a few books, a few keepsakes, and three monastic robes. It is a strong reminder that possessions do not make us happy.

We Are Not a Blank Sheet of Paper

PHAP HUU: I know I'm not perfect. I still allow myself to be carried away by the notion of self, but there are ways I keep myself grounded and in community. The back of the monastery kitchen is right outside my office, so I can see all the trash and recycling. Part of my practice is to clean up this area. This is a concrete action I can do that helps me to feel interbeing very directly.

Non-self can help us to understand that we have not come into this world like a blank sheet of paper—we are the result of all the causes and conditions of our ancestry, our culture, and the people in our proximity. To recognize these different influences, both those that have sustained us and those that have caused us suffering, it is helpful to embrace the energy of nonviolence. This is not just outward-looking nonviolence—it has to be directed inward. This means allowing silence to be present in our daily lives and slowing down to notice the machinations of our minds, to notice all the images that pop up without our conscious wish for them to be present.

In my case, I was introduced to porn at a very early age. All my cousins and uncles thought it was OK to pollute this young boy's mind, and I was submerged in pornographic images. Since becoming a monastic, I've experienced the total opposite. As monks, we live a celibate life, and we learn to take care of our sexual energy. I really struggled with that at the beginning—every time this energy came up, I judged myself as not being a pure monk. I even became very allergic to the word *purity* because I didn't think there was purity anywhere.

Rather than seeing particular actions as wrong, we can see them as our teachers and learn to transform them. As human beings, we're made of so many conditions. Each and every one of these conditions, if we embrace and accept them, can transform. I experienced a very special, healing moment with Thay when I was thirteen and had not yet become an ordained monk. Thay said, "Phap Huu, you're a teenager, you're going to experience changes in your body, in your feelings, in your energies. If you have any questions about sexual energy or you are uncertain what is happening in your body, please come to Thay. You can ask me."

This was a Zen master with a mission of bringing peace to the world, yet in this moment he attended fully to a young student on the cusp of accepting new changes in his body, emotions, and feelings. This memory continues to remind me of the importance of embracing and understanding ourselves—our bodies, minds, and all our emotions. Learning to love and accept ourselves may be a key to bringing about world peace.

Are You Sure?

PHAP HUU: In Zen, we talk about the superiority complex, the inferiority complex, and the equality complex. All three of them can be a barrier to being centered and stable in feeling we belong. If we really pay attention to the present moment, we can see all three complexes in play—the feeling of I'm better than, I'm less than, and I want to be treated exactly the same as someone else.

In the teachings of Buddhism, each of these three energies is a source of suffering: because we feel less than, we suffer; because we feel more than, we suffer—we may have a false impression of temporary happiness, but we suffer later and we suffer in feeling divided from those we believe we are better than; being treated exactly the same as everyone else, we suffer—we are not seen for our own character and history. Or we may suffer because we're convinced everyone should receive equal treatment and, as we know, this rarely happens. In the reality of non-self, we're all waves in the ocean. The wave in the ocean goes up, and the wave is happy, but it is just as happy when it rejoins the water. If the wave were to think like us, it may see another, bigger and stronger wave and no longer feel satisfied.

These three energies divide us because they lead to discrimination and create suffering in body, speech, and mind. These divisions manifest as racism and privilege and show up in the way we think, the way we perceive each other, and the way we interact. These complexes have their roots in our childhood and in what has been transmitted to us through our ancestors. We are often unaware of our tendencies to act in a certain way and may need the help of others to shine a light on our patterns of behavior.

If a wave has the insight of interbeing, it knows that at the core, waves are all water—it breaks free of all three of these complexes. Then the wave can be a very big wave and honor that it has all the conditions to be a big wave, or it can be a small wave without being jealous of a bigger wave. It can be happy just as it is.

To remember that without the support of our teachers, friends, and the natural world I cannot be who I am is a very concrete practice. Part of this is sharing our success, sharing what we are able to contribute, and seeing ourselves as part of a continuation. These practices transcend our feelings of superiority, inferiority, and equality.

If we are about to give a presentation, the complex of inferiority may arise in the belief that we do not have anything new or important to say. Or maybe we're feeling superior and believe that we are the ones with the answers and the audience just needs to do what we say. In either case, the Zen master would ask, *Are you sure?* If you are overconfident, he will ask if you are sure you have all the answers. *Are you sure you cannot be open and learn?* If you are feeling afraid, the Zen master will say, *Breathe my dear, you are enough.* If you feel you're always running and competing, always trying to be equal to everyone else, maybe the Zen voice will say, *Be beautiful, be yourself.*

Mindful Consumption

JO CONFINO: Being in the field of climate change and biodiversity loss, I am only too aware of the impacts of our overconsumption. But for many years, I noticed only the impacts of the products and services we buy, such as food, clothes, and energy. This aligns with the mainstream narrative that if we reduce our individual consumption by doing things like going vegetarian, avoiding fast fashion, and switching to renewable energy, we can stave off the worst effects of the climate and biodiversity crises.

The Plum Village teachings helped me develop a much broader understanding of consumption that includes what we feed our minds. In Zen, there are four ways we consume: through edible food, sense impressions, volition, and consciousness. This understanding points to how the way we consume products and services is driven by our thinking—the words, images and sounds we allow to enter our minds will influence our perceptions, judgments, views, and way of life. If we want to create fundamental change in our society, we must change our mindsets.

In our modern era, this may mean being more protective of our minds. With the development of AI, we have access to all of the world's knowledge, all the time. The Buddha reminded us that we are shaped by our thoughts; this means we should be very careful about how our thoughts are generated. We've all noticed how in thrall we are to our mobile phones. Recently, I burned a pan while cooking because I was reading the news on my phone at the same time. I followed the embedded links in the article down a rabbit hole and completely lost my sense of time and place, not to mention my mindfulness of what I was doing.

I am also aware of how living in a large city impacts us. Metropolises seem to have their own collective psychic energy; we are sensitive, and we can drown in it. When I lived in London, I took "the tube" (the subway) to work every day. As soon as I took the escalator down into the guts of the station, I would start to feel rushed—I could feel stress rising in me as though the energy of those around me resonated in my own body and mind. It reminded me of the film *Ghostbusters*, in which an underground river of slime runs through an old subway tunnel in New York. The slime, it turns out, was composed of all the negative emotions of the people living there.

Are we aware of the thoughts we produce every day and how these impact us individually as well as how they contribute to the consciousness of our family, our community, our society, and even the consciousness of our planet? We know there are lots of practical things we can do—like turn off our phone an hour before bed so we don't take the woes of the world into our sleep—but we also need to face the fact that the news and social media are structured to generate addictive behavior that can be difficult to counter.

PHAP HUU: We can reflect on this and be honest with ourselves about our addictions. Is it television? Is it music? Is it information? Once we know, we can start to switch what we consume and nourish ourselves with something more wholesome. We know, for example, that nature is a very good television—we can do more than just watch it, we can be in it. We develop addictions to self-soothe, because we feel there's nothing else to do.

If we always listen to dreadful news or engage in angry conversations, our seeds of fear will be watered—over time, we will become fearful and anxious. It's inevitable. The practice of taking care of ourselves involves being very mindful of what we expose ourselves to and recognizing that who we become is due to our consumption, and what we say or do will in turn be consumed by those around us.

As a practitioner and someone who wants to walk the path of contributing peace and understanding to the world, I have to recognize how I take care of what I consume in my daily life. I like to meditate on what I'm consuming and what I'm offering—to the people around me, to the environment, and to the whole world, the whole cosmos. Even those things that may appear to be mundane, such as sweeping and doing laundry, can be practices in which we find joy and freedom from anxiety. Who I am and who I become is what I give to the world.

We have to learn to recognize the energies in us, such as restlessness or dullness, and be honest about our habits. What is it that makes us turn away from the present moment? How can I nourish myself now? It may be connecting to a friend, writing, reading, or engaging in a hobby that feeds our spirit. Thay did calligraphy in his free time because it nourished his joy and brought his practice into the realm of art. Some of us love gardening. If you feel you can't change your habits on your own, find friends to support you. It's important to take it step by step—you can start by asking a friend to go for a walk together once a week.

BREATHER

"There is no need to be afraid to go home. At home, we can touch the most beautiful things. Home is in the present moment, the only moment we can touch life. If we do not go back to the present moment, how can we touch the beautiful sky, the sunset, or the eyes of our dear child? If we do not go home, how can we touch our heart, our lungs, our liver, and our eyes to give them a chance to be healthy? At home, we can touch all the wonders of life, the refreshing, beautiful, and healing elements."

Thich Nhat Hanh, 1994

CHAPTER 6

Practices to Return Home

Calm in the storm is not just an idea—it is something we live with our bodies, our breathing, and our presence. While insight can open the door to transformation, it is regular, grounded practice that gently carries us across the threshold. In this final section, we offer some of the most accessible and nourishing practices from the Plum Village tradition—simple tools to help you return to yourself, again and again.

These practices are not meant to be mastered or performed. They are invitations to slow down, to listen more deeply, to touch the stillness always available beneath the noise. Whether it's mindful breathing, walking meditation, pausing before picking up your phone, or simply sitting with your tea in silence, each act becomes a thread reconnecting you to your center.

Over time, these small moments of awareness become a refuge—a stable home you carry with you. When the winds of life rise, when the world feels uncertain, anxious, or overwhelming, these practices help you remain steady.

They are not separate from life—they are life, lived with intention and love.

A Foundation of Stillness

PHAP HUU: When we have the insight of interbeing, we start to understand the value of someone who is calm and solid, someone who is present, someone who has peace and the ability to listen without judging. If we're all busy, no one listens to each other. We're just showing off our sophisticated ideas, ideas we believe offer solutions, and our conversations quickly escalate into a battle of wills. This ego, that ego, wants to be seen, to be heard, to be loved.

If we look underneath, we see we are already what we want to become. Every action you take has an impact. Stop running after an image that is not you. Come back and embrace yourself. When you do that—how simple—you start healing your whole ancestral lineage.

Enlightenment does not come out of nowhere. It comes from the daily practice, the daily insight of simple actions. Yet a core practice in Zen is aimlessness. We can have a goal, but the goal is not our happiness. As a monk, I have an aspiration to offer retreats to help alleviate suffering and to make sure these retreats are the best they can be by deepening my practice and my understanding. But I don't wait until I'm enlightened to be happy. That is a wrong view. That's a view that carries us away from the present moment. When we prepare for a retreat, we cook together, we all clean the toilets. These are deep moments of togetherness. I don't wait until the end of the retreat to say this is happiness—already we are present, we are mindful, the offering is already here. We build a culture of continuous healing, transformation, and care. It's not a one-time action.

Simplicity embraces complexity. Getting stuck in complexity drives us further away from the foundation of stillness, the place in ourselves where we can be calm in any storm.

Sitting Meditation

PHAP HUU: To meditate is to be alive. To meditate is to connect. To meditate is to really feel that you are a miracle of life. By developing agency over our own breathing, we can strengthen deep looking and understanding, which in turn can give us a taste of freedom. Meditation allows us to be exactly how we are and who we are in this moment.

Like any other practice, it gets easier over time. Sitting meditation was hard for me when I first became a monk—we're all in the same boat. When I was young, I was never taught to sit still. I was never told how to feel the body, how to be aware of the mind. Arriving in Plum Village and making the decision to become an aspirant monk, I had to dive into the world of the monastics. In

Plum Village, sitting meditation takes place every morning and every evening. I confess: at the beginning, I just *forced* myself to sit on the cushion. There was little joy or freedom in it! The hardest part was just staying awake in the morning meditation—it was so early! I often fell asleep; I tried many techniques to stay awake. The most effective was sitting in full lotus sitting position—the sensation of pain in my legs kept me awake.

Our practice is a practice of nonviolence. Though we may have a perception that meditation means being still the entire time, giving yourself permission to bring ease into the body is important. When there is pain in sitting meditation, we can stretch our legs and release any tension that has built up. We can be flexible with our bodies and our breath in meditation. Be kind to yourself.

Over time, sitting meditation has become my foundation of stillness. It's like exercising: when you first start stretching, there's pain. When you start lifting weights or doing pull-ups, your muscles become sore. When I began meditating, the soreness was the agitation—the mind wanting me to move, wanting me to leave this hall. My mind often questioned me: *What are you doing here?* Exactly in those moments I got to hear myself and to identify the emotions that were present.

Sometimes we make the mistake of thinking our sitting seeks to achieve something, to do something. But meditation is *being*. The sitting is to be alive, to be very present. Our own ideas can get in the way of us thinking we have had a successful or fruitful meditation. We're so convinced there's something to do, that we're doing it wrong, and we don't allow ourselves to be as we are. Meditation is simply embracing and allowing us to be in the present moment in a really deeply attentive, curious way—it is the quality of our presence. With this perspective, I see how normal it was for me to fall asleep and to feel annoyed during meditation as a teenager—it was the first time in my young life I wasn't filling my days with video games and cartoons. After a childhood full of white noise, the silence became very powerful as I continued to sit in stillness with the Plum Village community.

We talk a lot in Plum Village about the power of presence. Sitting meditation is a cultivation of true presence. It is a practice of learning to simply be there for yourself. We give our suffering permission to be present and embrace it and care for it. We can even say to uncomfortable sensations: *Thanks to the stillness, you are being transformed by us.* As a teenager, I often felt like I wasn't doing anything when I meditated, and I wondered where the healing was that all the adults were talking about. Sitting meditation has ripened for me over time; I have come to recognize the healing of the moments of peace, calm, love, and presence I experience. I feel this energy palpably healing past wounds, including the lack of peace I touched from having been bullied or abused. The sitting is the healing, the sitting is the peace.

On a busy day, the sitting itself is purely to sit and do nothing. When you don't want to go sit is exactly when you need to go sit—these are moments when nobody will bother you. You can have thirty minutes of uninterrupted stillness. If you don't go sit, people will interrupt you. People will ask for your attention. You will get lost in emails, project planning, or whatever else is on your to-do list.

Practicing Meditation

I'd like to invite you into a meditation practice. Wherever you are, please begin by feeling the weight of your body. Become aware of your body. Begin to know you are here, to know you are breathing. You are alive. This is love. This is acceptance. Perhaps you can say, silently or out loud, *I am here for myself.*

As you sink into your body, feeling the weight, start to release any tension. If there is tension in your face, offer yourself a smile. If it's your shoulders that are tense, allow yourself to just put the burden down, put the worries down. If it's your arms, your fingers, your palms, maybe you've been holding onto something for so long. At this moment, just release it—it's not going to go anywhere, you can pick it back up later. For now, allow yourself to feel the relaxation of releasing the tension in your arms, your hands, your fingers. What are you grabbing onto?

Now, let us bring our awareness to our breath. I invite you to experiment with aligning the following phrases with your breath as a way to gather your attention:

> As I breathe in, I know I am breathing in. As I breathe out, I know I am breathing out. This is an in-breath. This is an out-breath.

Your mind may wander to the past, to the future, or to a story. Allow these thoughts to melt away. Allow yourself to just be with the breath. Let the mind gently come back to the body:

> Breathing in, I follow my in-breath from the beginning to the end. As I breathe out, I follow my out-breath from the beginning to the end. Feeling my abdomen rising and falling as I breathe in and out, my breath is life. I arrive deeper in my body; I arrive more deeply in the present moment.
>
> As I breathe in, I offer myself my true acceptance. As I breathe out, I smile with acceptance.
>
> Even if you didn't have the best day, even if you said something you still regret.
>
> I smile, I accept.
>
> I vow to speak more mindfully, more lovingly, and to act with compassion. If I am full of love, full of compassion, full of wellness, I can cultivate this and offer it to those around me.

Breathing in, I enjoy this present moment where life is happening. Breathing out, this is a wonderful moment. Breathing in, I am grateful that I am alive.

You have the conditions to breathe. You can walk. You can stand. You can eat. You can see. How wonderful it is to just be alive.

Breathing in, I smile to life with gratitude. Breathing out, I offer love.

It's okay to have a little bit of suffering.

Breathing in, I recognize my capacity. Breathing out, I give myself space. Breathing in, I am enough. Breathing out, I offer myself tenderness, kindness, and warmth. Breathing in, I accept myself. Breathing out, I smile.

Breathing in, I am in touch with all the wonders of life. Breathing out, I am grateful for all those wonders.

Walking Meditation

PHAP HUU: Walking meditation is a beautiful practice. Each and every one of us leaves marks on this beautiful planet each day. Our way of walking is a contribution. Our steps can embody what we aspire to. We know that with each step we are able to connect to Mother Earth, to this jewel in the universe. Isn't she so beautiful? If we see the wonders of life, we can change our way of living—we will want to protect Gaia, to love and care for her.

JO CONFINO: Paz, my wife, is a shining example of a disciplined meditation practitioner. She sits in our zendo every morning—sitting meditation is a fundamentally important part of her day. I find it difficult to sit on my own and much easier when I am part of a group. I also have not developed the suppleness in my body to be able to sit for long in comfort. It would be easy to be self-critical, to think my practice is not as accomplished as hers, but I have learned to be more compassionate with myself and with other people who may find a formal meditation practice difficult to maintain.

It is important to know what meditation is not. There is the old joke about people being late for their meditation or yoga class, arriving stressed and out of breath because they were rushing to be on time. There is another about people rushing around all day being stressed because they didn't have a perfect morning sitting.

We have to practice all day, every day. It is a way of life. It is good to remember that to practice is to stop and be present. While a formal practice can be very beneficial, we can also find periods of stillness when on a train or sitting in a traffic jam. If we look carefully, there are actually many moments during the day when we can allow ourselves to just be, such as sitting on a park bench watching the leaves of a tree rustling in the wind. Rather than seeing meditation as a once-a-day practice, it works better for me to introduce mindfulness into whatever

I do to better understand the machinations of my mind and transform my thinking as it arises.

I am grateful to Thay for the practice of walking meditation. He encouraged us to see that each moment of our ordinary lives is an opening for spiritual practice:

> Each mindful breath, each mindful step,
> reminds us that we are alive on this beautiful
> planet. We don't need anything else. It is wonderful enough just to be alive, to breathe in, and
> to make one step. We have arrived at where
> real life is available—the present moment. If
> we breathe and walk in this way, we become as
> solid as a mountain.

I can cultivate mindfulness when walking with much more ease than I can during silent sitting. There is something wonderful about aligning my steps with my breath and being outside and connecting to what is there, whether that means the land, the sky, the sun, the rain, or the wind.

Often, I accompany my in-breath and out-breath with a short poem Thay wrote specifically for this practice:

> I have arrived. I am home.
> In the here, in the now.
> I am solid, I am free.
> In the ultimate I dwell.

Breathing in, I say quietly to myself, "I have arrived" while I take four steps, and breathing out I say, "I am home" while I take five steps. Then I repeat the subsequent lines following the same pattern to align with my steps and my breath. Once I have finished the poem, I start again. You can make up your own poem or just use numbers as a way to connect your breath with your steps—whatever helps you to feel calm and present.

Walking meditation is particularly helpful when facing difficult emotions. When our mind is stirred up, it can be difficult to sit still, but walking mindfully can help to ease the mind and the body. This can be true for other movement practices as well. One of the Plum Village nuns, Sister True Dedication, says if sitting is too difficult, we can start with yoga, dance, or a deep relaxation practice:

> There are ways to come into the body that are more accessible in movement. In stillness, if the mind is overactive, it just takes over and won't establish a relationship with the body. There are other practice doors for many people who have an overactive mind. If we force our concentration, like we're trying to bend a metal bar to hold on to our inbreath and outbreath, we cause too much strain. In our tradition of Zen and this art of mindfulness, we wouldn't use that kind of force to concentrate the mind.

Breath

PHAP HUU: For those people who are at ease connecting to their breath, this is mindfulness itself. Taking refuge in each breath from the beginning all the way to the end, whether we are sitting in meditation or going about our daily life, develops presence. Nothing can interfere with this moment. We are truly present for our breath, truly present for ourselves. In the simple process of identifying our in-breath and out-breath and following their entire length, we develop two of the core Buddhist teachings: mindfulness and concentration. Together, these can generate new insights.

The breath helps bridge our mind and our body. You don't have to think about the breath as you feel the breath—the breath is already happening. By knowing you are breathing, you know you are here; because you are here, you have agency. By being present, we allow ourselves to be the best version of ourselves.

Following our breath is very important. Although we can be mindful, we can be aware, we may lose our mindfulness really quickly—we have the habit of thinking of the next thing already. It's like looking at a beautiful sunrise. As the sun starts to show itself, there is an awe, a feeling of *wow*. But we're so conditioned to quickly take it for granted, we often move on to think about the next thing within a few seconds, losing our connection to that moment.

Mindful concentration has transformed my sitting meditation—I recognize how quick I am to jump from topic to topic, from thought to thought, feeling uneasy and agitated. But when I have the foundation of my breath to take refuge in, every time a thought comes, I say, "I'm just going to stick with my in-breath from the beginning to the end." I start to develop stillness. This has translated throughout my whole life—whenever I am emotional, I feel my breath changing. When I'm agitated, my breath is very different. When I'm angry, my breath changes. By knowing my breath, I know myself. By making the connection between our emotions and our breathing, we can accompany whatever emotion is arising and not allow it to hijack our awareness.

Allow your breath to become your foundation of being in each moment. The breath is the fundamental place to take refuge in. It shines the light of mindfulness on what is happening inside of us and around us. We don't suppress anger; we don't suppress irritation; we identify the feeling: *I'm irritated right now.* If you cannot identify your breath, don't even think about identifying your feelings and emotions.

The power of mindful breathing is that you don't lose yourself. If anything, you allow yourself to be truly here for exactly what is happening. You aren't hijacked by the mind, by emotions, or by feelings. The breath is a thread of seeing, thinking, and saying things more compassionately. Essentially, as a meditator, this is what we want to bring to the table in every connection: understanding, compassion, and love.

Body

PHAP HUU: One of the first benefits of meditation is as simple and as difficult as being able to come back to your body. We can learn to be at ease with our body, to accept it as it is right now, but with the expansiveness of knowing we are not limited to this one moment—we continuously evolve and change. We are not conditioned only by what is happening in the world around us; we also have the capacity to condition ourselves. This is part of the journey of arriving home, of redeveloping our foundation of stability and calm in any storm.

For many of us, our biggest practice is to accept ourselves as we are. The practice of smiling to ourselves can be the deepest practice. Normally our smiles are aimed at other people. Have we ever just smiled to ourselves? Have we ever smiled to our own body or to the discomfort we experience? Often, we suppress, we look for a way out—for example, we consume—because we don't want to be with our body.

The power of coming home to the body is the insight that you're alive. Just knowing you have a body is insight—much of the time, our mind and our body don't communicate well. Calming the body is very soothing:

aware of our body as we breathe in, relaxing our body as we breathe out. Our breathing and our body are interconnected.

My body has become my bell of mindfulness. My body is a great communicator, letting me know what is going on. It can tell me if I am feeling tense, and then I can put my hand on my abdomen for support. We have a tradition in Plum Village called a *body scan*, which involves mentally going through our body and thanking each organ and body part for supporting our life. I thank my eyes for allowing me to see so much beauty in the world, my nose for its ability to smell, my mouth for the joy of taste, and my ears for listening to all the sounds of the world. I focus on my hands, my arms, my legs, and then each of my organs, my heart, my lungs, my liver, and so on, expressing my appreciation. If there is a part that hurts, I send my attention to that part of the body to comfort it. This gives me a lot of energy in the morning. When I wake up, I start the day with gratitude for my body—then the rest of the day can unfold.

Head on a Stick

JO CONFINO: If I am honest with myself, for most of my life I have found it difficult to connect to my body. My upbringing valued the mind—not the body. In fact, I was rather ashamed of my body. The last thing I wanted to do was listen to it. I would rather it had just gone away.

I have come to realize that when I focus only on my thoughts, it is very difficult to allow my body to give me insights into my feelings or to allow my heart to speak with me. I am by no means alone in this. The most extreme example I have come across of this was while coaching a board director of a global bank. He shared that he had completely lost himself in the daily machinations of his demanding work schedule and did not have the time to feel into what was going on in his life. He was on an eternal treadmill, he said, mechanically solving one problem after another. He graphically described himself as "a head on a stick," not even aware he had a body.

He had come to me because he had gone beyond his limits and experienced a breakdown. He recognized his mind and body could no longer carry him—a fundamental reset was necessary. It likely won't come as a surprise at this point that part of his healing journey involved slowing down and letting go of some of his responsibilities so he could truly recognize that he lived in his body; it was not separate from him. Luckily, for him to reconnect his mind and body was as simple as going for a walk and allowing his body to speak to him.

Coming Home to This Moment

PHAP HUU: We don't just heal for ourselves. We heal for the collective. We have to expand our mind and expand ourselves to see that our suffering is not ours alone—it is a shared suffering. We don't discriminate between small transformation and big transformation. All transformations impact the consciousness of our society. When we talk about coming home to ourselves, about finding calm in the storm and cultivating stability, we have a foundation: learning to be in the present moment, the moment in which our healing takes place.

Our responsibility is to learn to be in the present moment and dwell happily in it. Sometimes we have wrong perceptions of the word *happy*—I know I did. Early in my training to be a monk, I thought I had to be happy to be in the present moment. Over time I understood happiness to mean not discriminating between experiencing a storm inside or a blissful moment. In every situation, if we look deeply, we see we have enough conditions to be happy. If this is a moment of suffering, I can still be there for this moment. I can generate happiness in this moment, even in the midst of suffering and pain.

The present moment is where life is happening. It takes practice to be present for the moment happening now; time is always flowing. Right now, this very moment is the present moment. But it quickly becomes the past, and the next moment moves out of the future. The present moment, though, is all around us. How our life is, right here, is the present moment. Your breath is the present moment. Gratitude is the present moment.

Awareness of a tree can be the present moment. The present moment holds everything, but it depends on how we can cultivate that present moment.

One of our elders, Sister Jina, speaks so eloquently about the present moment. She says that if we truly realize this is the only moment we have, we will live our lives differently. We may not spend time thinking what we're thinking. We may not say what we're about to say. We may not do what we're about to do. We will interact with others in a different way. But most of us live as if we and those around us will live forever.

One of the ways we can be invited back to the present moment is by listening to the sound of a bell. In Plum Village, whenever we hear the sound of a bell, whether it is the great temple bell or the chiming clock in the dining hall, we stop. We don't just stop physically, but also in our minds. When we stop, we relax and let go of what is crowding our mind, what is preoccupying us, what is tearing us away from the present moment. Over time, this relaxation, this stopping, comes naturally. You don't need to be in a monastery to practice this. Many apps, including our own Plum Village app, have a downloadable bell that we can set, or as we say, invite to ring at regular intervals.

We often get stuck in a particular way of thinking, but we change in every moment. Each day is an opportunity.

In renewing the present moment, we can help renew the past. If we are lucky, the past was very beautiful, full of care and love. For some, the past was very challenging, full of difficulty, violence, pain, and hurt. If we know how to be in this present moment, how to be a painter painting this present moment, we can transform the past. By taking agency in this very moment, we can heal our wounds from the past and create a new past.

Our present moment has another beautiful capacity—it creates our path forward, creates the future we aspire to be in. If we would like to become more calm and more stable, we have to be real. We can't just wish for it. We have been offered the path of mindful breathing. Every moment we are alive is a gift, an invitation to come back to the breath, to connect to this breath and to the wonders of life. If you find yourself in despair and fear, not knowing what to rely on, look inward. Anchor yourself in your breath.

BREATHER
A Present Moment Practice by Sister Jina

If you hear your phone ring or a notification alert come in, do not rush to find which pocket our phone is in and then answer in a stressed way.

Instead, take a moment to become aware of your in-breath and out-breath. Life is happening now. We can become aware of our body. Are we tense? We can become aware of our state of mind. Are we able, with an out-breath, to let go of what is preoccupying us? Can we be truly present when we listen to the caller's voice or view an incoming message?

We can already tell by the sound of the person's voice or the tone of a message whether happiness is present or not. We don't know what kind of support the person trying to reach us might need. If we are calm, whatever they ask, we can respond from a place of presence. Will the other person feel heard and understood?

If everybody would just do this, the world would already be a much better, more compassionate place. We all have the capacity to be present. We do not need to study extensively, we don't need to read a pile of books—if we become aware of our breathing and relax, we see what is happening within and around us more clearly, and we will interact more appropriately, more skillfully, in any situation.

Connecting to Ancestors

PHAP HUU: One aspect of reconnecting to life is recognizing that sometimes our suffering is a transmission from our ancestors. If they were unable to recognize and transform suffering in their own lives, it gets passed on. It's like when a child is brought up in a family who uses cuss words on a daily basis—the child will just naturally start speaking like that, whether they think it is correct or not. I speak from personal experience: one of my uncles was an alcoholic, and he cussed every three sentences or so. I grew up to do the same, dropping F-bombs simply because that habit was transmitted to me by my environment.

We are conditioned in our way of speaking, our way of thinking, and our way of acting based on what we receive. There is a core of suffering that we receive. Even if you are brought up in a very well-off family where the conditions look good from the outside, there are likely to be particular knots and holes that haven't yet surfaced, and suffering that will also be transmitted to you. These individual, ancestral, and cultural forces shape us—they deeply impact and mold our mind consciousness.

Touching the Earth

PHAP HUU: We have a practice in Plum Village called Touching the Earth, during which we bow to the ground out of respect and love for our teachers.[11] We start by bringing our hands together, symbolizing the joining of our body and mind, and then we bring our palms to our forehead, signifying an invitation to all of our ancestors, spiritual and blood, to be present in us. When we touch the earth, they touch the earth with us. We bow down, allowing our forehead to touch the ground, and open our palms upward to show there is nothing to hide. It is a gesture of opening our hearts, being true to ourselves, letting our ancestors be present, and aspiring to something new.

We offer four gratitudes during touching the earth to get in touch with the truth that we are not separate individuals but inter-are with everyone and everything else. By connecting in this way, we honor our lineage, our blood and spiritual ancestors. When we light up our own aspirations, we also light up the aspirations of our ancestors, some of whom may not have had the opportunity to develop a spiritual life. We also practice for them.

The first gratitude is for our parents, the ones who brought us life. Just knowing we are alive is a gift. Maybe our parents suffered and did not have the right conditions to cultivate a feeling of peace. But we can cultivate it for them. We can transform their suffering in our practice. Our happiness is also their happiness.

The second gratitude is for all the teachers who have taught us how to love and generate true understanding.

For me, of course, I connect to Thay, who opened a path for me to walk. In that moment, I can connect to his presence rather than seeing him as outside of me. When I practice, he lives on through me. We bring all our spiritual teachers into our awareness, and our gratitude enhances our motivation to practice.

The third gratitude is for our friends on the path, everyone who has supported us through difficult as well as joyful moments. By honoring them, we cultivate the quality of friendship in us and in others around us.

The last gratitude is for the whole cosmos, the earth, and all living beings. We thank the trees for giving us air to breathe, we appreciate the rain for providing the water for our tea or coffee, we thank the sun for offering us light and warmth. Even if things don't always feel perfect, we can touch so much gratitude. With gratitude, our lives become richer, and we feel more fulfilled. We touch calmness and stability.

CHAPTER 7

True Presence

Bringing Our Practice into the World

PHAP HUU: Our way of taking action has an impact in daily life—on our loved ones, our family, our community, our nation, and the world. When we have wisdom, we ask how we can contribute to positive change. It is most helpful to think not about what we can do as an individual, but how we contribute to a collective awakening.

For the polycrisis we are facing, we need multitudes of bodhisattvas—selfless beings who understand that the well-being of the planet is no different from their well-being, that the well-being of those living in distant lands is their own well-being. If you're really present when you hear or read the news, it's impossible not to suffer. If you don't suffer, you're running away from reality.

The core practice is to recognize suffering without drowning in it or being a victim of the suffering—to embrace, accept, and see what to do and what not to do. This is meditation. This is how we integrate the spiritual dimension into daily life—by recognizing, embracing, seeing the changes that need to happen, and then being that change. If we know how to recognize our suffering, understand our suffering, and take care of our suffering, we give it a chance to transform. That is wellness. That is inner strength. That is calm in any storm.

We often have the tendency to want others to change without being prepared to change ourselves. The practice of mindfulness brings the responsibility back to oneself. The first practice is to listen. Sometimes we become so sure, and we think there is only one way; we can be very dogmatic about it. We must listen and then learn to share compassionately, using language to build bridges, harmony, and common purpose while still respecting the different paths we take.

We have held retreats for climate leaders around the world for a number of years. For the first three days of these retreats, we ask the participants to please trust us and just invest time to be with yourself. We acknowledge that they may feel a little bit guilty about it, but assure them that it is so crucial—the actions we want to create must be based on love, care, and healing. If we can't touch these things inside of ourselves, how can we offer them to the world?

When we speak about coming back to oneself, it's not about taking care of the ego. It's about finding the beautiful conditions inside that we want to cultivate outside.

Then we have the ingredients to offer to our loved ones, friends, colleagues, and to everyone we encounter. What is most important is to offer our presence. Start with those closest to you, whom you feel comfortable with, and see change start to happen—healing starts to happen. From that experience, faith will grow; you will see it work on a small scale and believe it can also work on a larger scale.

In the early years of becoming a monk, my capacity was very limited. The amount of suffering I could listen to without overreacting and being extremely tense in my body was limited. Over time, I have become aware enough to know I can always take refuge in my breath. Even though what is being shared may be deeply painful, instead of drowning and being overwhelmed by sorrow, I am held by the foundation of my breathing. I'm present with the suffering, but I can guide it. This kind of inner work is so necessary today—what we are facing will bring up intense despair and grief. We all need a place of refuge, and we need communities. Community is the way forward. We cannot do it by ourselves. There's no superman who will suddenly appear and change the situation. We need a collective movement, a collective awakening, a collective practice.

When I made tea for Thay for the first time after becoming his attendant, I was very eager to make him the absolute best cup of tea. As I poured the hot water over the new tea leaves, I wanted to pour a cup right away to offer to Thay, but he said, "Stop, let the tea sit. Everything that does sitting meditation is better. Allow the tea to sit for at least two minutes so the fragrance, the true essence of the tea, will manifest. Everything that takes time will offer its best." Allowing all things to offer their true essence in life has since become my goal.

The mind is the base of how we create our world. We live in a culture where we like to make things more sophisticated than they should be and there is ego to that. If it sounds too simple, nobody believes it can help solve the climate emergency or contribute to world peace. There is a saying, *Don't just sit there, do something*. Thay reversed that: *Don't just do something, sit there*. Sitting there doesn't mean doing nothing. Sitting there means looking deeply at the causes of our suffering. By doing so, we can start to untangle the complexity of our situation.

When we're not able to sit still and connect to life, we continue to add layers of complexity to our suffering. This is why the first wing of meditation is learning to pause, learning to slow down. When an animal is wounded, it knows how to stop, rest, and heal. We have this idea that by sitting still and "doing nothing," we're not contributing. Conversely, we think it is only by doing that we make a contribution. Sometimes, of course, this is correct, but sometimes our action is based not on an insight of healing and transformation, but on a wish to cover something up, to avoid something. This collective habit has become part of our culture.

In a world that urges constant motion, the practice of pausing—of sitting, breathing, and coming home to ourselves—is itself a radical act. It allows us to see clearly, to act with compassion rather than reactivity, and to nourish the seeds of understanding and transformation. True engagement with the world begins not in grand gestures, but in small, steady moments of presence at critical times. When we touch the stillness within, we begin to touch the world with more care. From this grounded place, our actions—no matter how humble—can become part of a collective awakening. This is how we bring our practice into the world: not to escape its suffering, but to meet it with clarity, resilience, and love.

Walking This Path Together

JO CONFINO: We cannot find anything outside of ourselves that is not already in ourselves. Our consciousness shifts and shapes our world. Our thoughts create our reality and when we have the courage to change our patterns of belief and action, the world cannot help but also change.

Thay describes us as artists "painting every phenomenon into being." It's such a simple, profound truth, yet it can be a challenge to integrate into our lives and we often feel a victim of circumstance, much less the artist of our own life. It can sometimes feel like we wrestle with this realization: as soon as we have a grip on it, it slips away and settles at the edge of our horizon.

Rather than feeling demoralized about this, we can learn to cherish and to celebrate the moments when we pierce through the fog and see life with depth and clarity. We are constantly offered the choice to love or hate, to blame or forgive, to fight or accept. Knowing a light is always shining, showing us the way, is balm to the soul.

We come into this world and into our adulthood with a lot of baggage that can weigh us down. Some people suffer traumas that crush their spirit, yet we all have the capacity to start healing our wounds if we are able to summon courage and seek support. The deeper the pain, the more deeply we can touch the beauty of life. *No mud, no lotus.*

When we stop for a moment, we can see that life is a great adventure. It may not have the swashbuckling nature of a Hollywood action movie, but in our search for meaning we are able to touch and be enchanted by both magic and mystery.

The most effective way we accumulate wisdom and develop a sense of stability in our lives is knowing we have the capacity to come home to ourselves, to come home to life, to rest our weary minds and bodies and find calm in any storm. There is nothing quite as life-affirming as the ability to touch peace. When we feel revived and centered, we have greater resilience to face the many challenges of the world. Even in the midst of chaos, we can find moments of calm and ease. From this place of belonging, we can be a light to others and illuminate their path just by offering our presence.

On the most profound level, we all walk this path together, from generation to generation, continuing far into the future. We hope this book offers you some sustenance that can support you as you take the next calm step on this extraordinary journey we call life.

Appreciation

Human civilization has gone through many dark periods. What can help us to remain calm and maintain our trust in difficult times is knowing of courageous people through the ages who found the strength and resilience to act even in the midst of despair. First and foremost, I would like to express my appreciation for all those who have transmitted the true power of action that is driven by compassion and love. It is on their shoulders that we stand.

We live in a VUCA—volatile, uncertain, complex and ambiguous—world, and I have found great strength and rootedness in the endlessly deep teachings of Thich Nhat Hanh. They have allowed me to maintain my footing, even when the terrain of my life has been steep and uneven. I also have enormous gratitude for the monks and nuns of Plum Village, who keep the flame of wisdom burning and provide a true refuge for thousands of people every year around the world.

Brother Phap Huu is a shining example of what it means to be in service to the world, and he is wise beyond his years. It is an honor and a pleasure to have written our second book together and to be jointly recording *The Way Out Is In* podcast series.

I am ever thankful to my wife, Paz Perlman, for her extraordinary support, wisdom, and unconditional love. She introduced me to the Plum Village teachings, and I continue to be inspired by her deep search for meaning and healing through her art practice and her mindful way of living. To my two sons and all my siblings: I know you are there, and I am very happy.

The team at Parallax Press has shown extraordinary generosity, dedication, and professionalism in bringing this book to fruition. I am also very appreciative of my friend Sarah Sallman for reading the draft manuscript and offering valuable feedback.

Two women have been beacons in my life: my mother, Lore, and the eco-philosopher and Buddhist scholar Joanna Macy. My mother, in her later years, found the inner strength to transcend the horrors of Nazism and to go back to Germany and offer forgiveness and reconciliation. She showed me the art of the possible. Joanna has inspired me over many years; in one of our podcast episodes, she touched me deeply when she said this moment of great danger in the world is not a place to dwell only in sorrow, but represents the greatest time to be alive, since we have the chance to individually and collectively carve out a new path of love. Lore and Joanna never knew each other, but their love for the German poet Rainer Maria

Rilke connected them across space and time; they both translated some of his works. In honor of them both, here is an impromptu translation Joanna recited for me of Rilke's of "Dear Darkening Ground," which speaks to this moment in our history.

> Dear darkening ground,
> You've endured so patiently the walls we've built.
> Please grant the cities one more hour
>
> And the churches and cloisters, maybe give them two
>
> And those that labor—let their work still grip them
>   for another five hours, or seven,
> before you become water and widening wilderness
>   and waste
> in that hour of inconceivable terror
> when you take back your name from all things.
>
> Just give me a little more time!
>
> I just wanted a little more time because I am going to
>   love the things
>
> as no one has thought to love them,
> until they're real. And worthy. And cherished.[12]

Combining everyone and everything I care for, I would like to express my deep gratitude to life. As Thay said, the miracle is not to walk on water but to walk on this precious earth.

Notes

1. For more on the Four Noble Truths and other foundational Buddhist teachings, see Thich Nhat Hanh, *The Heart of the Buddha's Teaching: Transforming Suffering into Peace, Joy, and Liberation* (Riverhead, 1999).
2. Stephen Mitchell, *Tao Te Ching* (HarperCollins, 1982).
3. Joanna Macy, in Brother Phap Huu and Jo Confino, hosts, *The Way Out Is In*, season 1, episode 12, https://plumvillage.org/podcast/grief-and-joy-on-a-planet-in-crisis-joanna-macy-on-the-best-time-to-be-alive-episode-12.
4. W. S. Merwin, "Place," in *The Rain in the Trees* (Alfred A. Knopf, 1988), 63.
5. "The Five Remembrances" in Thich Nhat Hanh and the Monks and Nuns of Plum Village, *Chanting from the Heart Volume 2: Ceremonies and Practices in the Plum Village Tradition*, (Parallax Press, 2023), 228.
6. Thich Nhat Hanh, *The Art of Power: A Zen Master's Guide to Redefining Power, Achieving True Freedom and Discovering Lasting Happiness in a Stressful World* (HarperOne, 2008), 103.
7. Paulo Coelho, *The Alchemist* (HarperCollins, 1995).
8. Nguyen Du, *The Song of Kieu: A New Lament* (Penguin Classics) translated by Timothy Allen, Penguin, 2019).

9. Thich Nhat Hanh, *The Heart of the Buddha's Teaching: Transforming Suffering into Peace, Joy, and Liberation* (Riverhead, 1999), 250.
10. Sister Chan Khong, *Beginning Anew: Four Steps to Restoring Communication* (Parallax Press, 2015).
11. Thich Nhat Hanh, *Touching the Earth: Guided Meditations for Mindfulness Practice* (Parallax Press, 2004).
12. Poem recited to author Jo Confino on Brother Phap Huu and Jo Confino, hosts, *The Way Out Is In*, season 1, episode 12, https://plumvillage.org/podcast/grief-and-joy-on-a-planet-in-crisis-joanna-macy-on-the-best-time-to-be-alive-episode-12. An earlier translation can be read in Rainer Maria Rilke, *The Book of Hours: Love Poems to God*, trans. Anita Barrows and Joanna Macy (Riverhead Books, 1996), 153.

About the Authors

BROTHER PHAP HUU (DHARMA FRIEND) first encountered Zen Master Thich Nhat Hanh and the Plum Village community as a nine-year-old child when he traveled from Canada to Plum Village France in 1996 with his father and sister. He was immediately drawn by the joyous brotherhood and the peaceful comportment of the monks. At the age of twelve, he knew then that he wished to become a monk. After much persistence on his part, his family allowed him to realize this wish at the age of thirteen. Brother Phap Huu was ordained as a novice monk in 2002. He received full bhikkhu ordination on December 18, 2006, and the Lamp Transmission as a Dharma Teacher in 2009. He became vice abbot in 2008 and has been the abbot of Upper Hamlet since January 2011, at the age of twenty-three. He was Thich Nhat Hanh's personal attendant for seventeen years. As an abbot, Brother Phap Huu takes his time to connect with and understand his monastic and lay brothers. He is much appreciated as a skillful facilitator at Sangha gatherings. His favorite practices are walking meditation and organizing retreats in Plum Village. He is interested in team building, coaching, and mentoring. When playing, Brother Phap Huu loves basketball and music.

JO CONFINO is a leadership coach, spiritual mentor, facilitator, journalist, author, and sustainability expert. He works at the intersection of personal transformation and systems change and his coaching practice focuses on supporting leaders within the fields of climate, biodiversity and social justice. As a journalist for more than forty years, he was executive editor as well as Impact, Innovation, and editorial director of What's Working at the *HuffPost* in New York. Before joining *HuffPost*, he was an executive editor of *The Guardian*, helping to create the environment, sustainable business, and global development websites as well as being responsible for ensuring the media organization lived its own values. A mindfulness advocate, Jo has worked closely with Zen Master Thich Nhat Hanh and his monastic community in southwestern France for nearly twenty years.

About *The Way Out Is In* Podcast

This podcast series is aimed at helping us to transcend our fear and anger so we can be more engaged in the world in a way that develops love and compassion. Thich Nhat Hanh's calligraphy "The Way Out Is In" highlights that the way out of any difficulty is to look deeply into our suffering, gain insights on how to transform our lives, and then to integrate the simple yet profound practices that sustain us. *The Way Out is In* is co-hosted by Brother Phap Huu and Jo Confino and is co-produced by the Plum Village App and Global Optimism, with support from the Thich Nhat Hanh Foundation.

Monastics and visitors practice the art of mindful living in the tradition of Thich Nhat Hanh at our mindfulness practice centers around the world. To reach any of these communities, or for information about how individuals, couples, and families can join in a retreat, please contact:

PLUM VILLAGE
24240 Thénac, France
plumvillage.org

LA MAISON DE L'INSPIR
77510 Villeneuve-sur-Bellot, France
maisondelinspir.org

HEALING SPRING MONASTERY
77510 Verdelot, France
healingspringmonastery.org

MAGNOLIA GROVE MONASTERY
Batesville, MS 38606, USA
magnoliagrovemonastery.org

BLUE CLIFF MONASTERY
Pine Bush, NY 12566, USA
bluecliffmonastery.org

DEER PARK MONASTERY
Escondido, CA 92026, USA
deerparkmonastery.org

EUROPEAN INSTITUTE OF APPLIED BUDDHISM
D-51545 Waldbröl, Germany
eiab.eu

THAILAND PLUM VILLAGE
*Nakhon Ratchasima
30130 Thailand*
thaiplumvillage.org

ASIAN INSTITUTE OF APPLIED BUDDHISM
Lantau Island, Hong Kong
pvfhk.org

STREAM ENTERING MONASTERY
*Porcupine Ridge, Victoria 3461
Australia*
nhapluu.org

MOUNTAIN SPRING MONASTERY
Bilpin, NSW 2758, Australia
mountainspringmonastery.org

For more information visit: *plumvillage.org*
To find an online sangha visit: *plumline.org*
For more resources, try the Plum Village app: *plumvillage.app*
Social media: *@thichnhathanh @plumvillagefrance*

THICH NHAT HANH FOUNDATION

planting seeds of Compassion

THE THICH NHAT HANH FOUNDATION works to continue the mindful teachings and practice of Zen Master Thich Nhat Hanh, in order to foster peace and transform suffering in all people, animals, plants, and our planet. Through donations to the Foundation, thousands of generous supporters ensure the continuation of Plum Village practice centers and monastics around the world, bring transformative practices to those who otherwise would not be able to access them, support local mindfulness initiatives, and bring humanitarian relief to communities in crisis in Vietnam.

By becoming a supporter, you join many others who want to learn and share these life-changing practices of mindfulness, loving speech, deep listening, and compassion for oneself, each other, and the planet.

For more information on how you can help support mindfulness around the world, or to subscribe to the Foundation's monthly newsletter with teachings, news, and global retreats, visit tnhf.org.

PARALLAX PRESS, a nonprofit publisher founded by Zen Master Thich Nhat Hanh, publishes books and media on the art of mindful living and Engaged Buddhism. We are committed to offering teachings that help transform suffering and injustice. Our aspiration is to contribute to collective insight and awakening, bringing about a more joyful, healthy, and compassionate society.

View our entire library at parallax.org.

THE MINDFULNESS BELL is a journal of the art of mindful living in the Plum Village tradition of Thich Nhat Hanh. To subscribe or to see the worldwide directory of Sanghas (local mindfulness groups), visit mindfulnessbell.org.